TEACHER'S PET PUBLICATIONS

LITPLAN TEACHER PACK
for
Medea
based on the play by
Euripides

Written by
Elizabeth Osborne

© 2010 Teacher's Pet Publications
All Rights Reserved

Copyright Teacher's Pet Publications 2010

Only the student materials in this unit plan (such as worksheets, study questions, and tests) may be reproduced multiple times for use in the purchaser's classroom.

For any additional copyright questions, contact Teacher's Pet Publications.

www.tpet.com

TABLE OF CONTENTS – *Medea*

About the Author	4
Introduction	5
Unit Objectives	8
Reading Assignment Sheet	9
Unit Outline	10
Study Questions (Short Answer)	13
Quiz/Study Questions (Multiple Choice)	19
Vocabulary Worksheets	31
Lesson One (Introductory Lesson)	49
Non-fiction Assignment Sheet	53
Oral Reading Evaluation Form	61
Writing Assignment 1	77
Writing Evaluation Form	78
Writing Assignment 2	83
Discussion Questions	87
Vocabulary Review Activities	89
Unit Review Activities	90
Writing Assignment 3	93
Unit Tests	97
Unit Resource Materials	145
Vocabulary Resource Materials	167

ABOUT THE AUTHOR

Euripides

Euripides (480 BC – 406 BC) was one of the three greatest ancient Greek tragedians (along with Aeschylus and Sophocles). Very little is known about his life, but more of his plays survive than those by other Greek playwrights.

Euripides is known for the psychological realism of his characters. Medea, for instance, expresses a wide range of very complicated human emotions, including jealousy, resentment, self-pity, and love. What is more, Euripides' audience, like his characters, may have trouble coming to an emotional conclusion about some of the very difficult issues the playwright raises. Medea has the right to be angry, but it is hard to agree with the actions that result from this anger. There are no clear answers about how justice should be administered.

Euripides also raises questions about the treatment of foreigners and women within Greek society. In the *Bacchae*, the god Dionysus, son of Zeus, fights for recognition as a deity. His worshipers are looked down upon because they come from Asia Minor instead of Greece. Medea's rights as both a woman and a foreigner are limited; her husband discards her and marries a Greek princess.

Euripides is famous for his use of the "deus ex machina" ("god from the machine"), a device that neatly but unrealistically resolves the problems of the plot. For instance, in the play *Ion*, the goddess Athena descends and explains away the complications of the plot. Euripides was criticized by his contemporaries for his repeated use of this device.

In Euripides' time, plays were written for entry into competitions at festivals like the *Dionysia*. The *Dionysia* was a large religious festival held in honor of the god Dionysus (the god of both wine and the theater). Euripides won the first prize in 441 BC and then three more times. In comparison, Aeschylus is said to have won fourteen times, and Sophocles more than twenty.

Major Works
Eighteen plays by Euripides survive. Part of a manuscript containing the plays of Euripides in alphabetical order was discovered in a monastery; the works that have titles that start with the Greek equivalent of the letters E-K remain.

Euripides' most famous plays are *Medea, The Trojan Women, Electra*, and *The Bacchae*.

Awards
Euripides won first prize at the City Dionysia for his tragedies in 441, 425, and 405 BC (when his plays were performed posthumously).

INTRODUCTION *Medea*

This unit has been designed to develop students' reading, writing, thinking, and language skills through exercises and activities related to *Medea* by Euripides. It includes twenty lessons, supported by extra resource materials.

The two **introductory lessons** introduce students to Greek theater, the organization of Greek plays, and the mythological background of *Medea*. At the end of the second lesson, students begin the pre-reading work for the first reading assignment. Before they actually begin to read the play, students respond to a brief journal prompt that prepares them for the emotional states of the characters in the opening scenes of *Medea*.

The **reading assignments** are done for homework, followed by oral readings in class. The parts to be spoken during each class period are listed in the lessons. The teacher needs only to assign students to each part. Students have approximately fifteen minutes of work to do prior to each reading assignment. This pre-reading work involves reviewing the study questions for the assignment and doing vocabulary work for three to ten vocabulary words they will encounter during their reading.

The **study guide questions** are fact-based; students can find the answers to these questions right in the text. The questions come in two formats: short answer and multiple-choice. The best use of these materials is to use the short answer version of the questions as study guides for students (since answers will be more complete), and use the multiple-choice version for occasional quizzes. If your school has the appropriate equipment, it might be a good idea to make transparencies of your answer keys for the overhead projector.

The **vocabulary work** is intended to enrich students' vocabularies as well as aid in the students' understanding of the play. Prior to each reading assignment, students will complete a two-part worksheet for approximately three to ten words in the upcoming reading assignment. Part I focuses on students' use of general knowledge and contextual clues by giving the sentence in which the word appears in the text. Students are then to write down what they think the words mean based on the words' usage. Part II reinforces understanding of the words by giving students dictionary definitions of the words and having them match the words to the correct definitions based on the words' contextual usage. Students should then have a thorough knowledge of the words when they encounter them in the text.

After each reading assignment, students will go back and formulate answers for the study guide questions. Discussion of these questions serves as a review of the most important events and ideas presented in the reading assignments.

After students complete reading the work, there is a **vocabulary review** lesson which pulls together all the vocabulary lists for the reading assignments and gives students a review of the words they have studied.

The **group activity** which follows the vocabulary review has students working in small groups to discuss several important aspects of the play. Using the information they have acquired so far through individual work and class discussions, students get together to further examine the text and to brainstorm ideas relating to five specific aspects of the play.

The group activity is followed by a **reports and discussion** session in which the groups share their ideas about their topics with the class; thus, the entire class is exposed to information about all the topics and can discuss each topic based on the nucleus of information brought forth by each of the groups.

Two lessons are devoted to **creating a film version** of *Medea* based on the knowledge students have gained, their personal feelings and experiences, and the needs of a modern audience.

A lesson is devoted to the **extra discussion questions/writing assignments**. These questions focus on interpretation, critical analysis and personal response, employing a variety of thinking skills and adding to the students' understanding of the play.

There are three **writing assignments** in this unit, each with the purpose of informing, interpreting, or having students express personal opinions. The first assignment is to inform: students write a composition based upon their theme topics. The second assignment is interpretive: students recast dialogues from *Medea* using modern methods of communication. The topic is given in the letter assignment. The third assignment is to give students a chance to simply express their own opinions: following the unit test, students write a composition explaining who, in their opinion, is the most sympathetic character in *Medea*.

In addition, there is a **Greek history research assignment**. Students are required to fill out a sheet of terms related to 5th-century BC Greece and then find an article or section of a nonfiction work on one of the topics (philosophy, ancient tragedy, the Persian or Peloponnesian Wars, Greek art and architecture, Athenian democracy, etc.). During one class period, students make **oral presentations** about the topics they have researched. This not only exposes all students to a wealth of information, it also gives them the opportunity to practice **public speaking**.

There is a **nonfiction reading assignment** that accompanies the Greek history assignment. In the process of researching the Greek history assignment, each student will fill out a worksheet about one of the articles, chapters, etc. he or she read as part of the research. On the worksheet, the students answer questions regarding facts, interpretation, criticism, and personal opinions. This gives them practice analyzing nonfiction sources.

The **review lesson** pulls together all the aspects of the unit. There is a choice of four to five activities or games to use, which all serve the same basic function of reviewing all the information presented in the unit.

The **unit test** comes in two formats: short answer and multiple-choice. In addition, each format has matching, quotations, composition, and vocabulary sections. As a convenience, two different tests for each format have been included.

There are additional **support materials** included with this unit. The **extra activities packet** includes suggestions for an in-class library, crossword and word search puzzles related to the play, and extra vocabulary worksheets. There is a list of **bulletin board ideas** which provides suggestions for bulletin boards to go along with this unit. In addition, there is a list of **extra class activities** to choose from to enhance this unit or as a substitution for an exercise the teacher might feel is inappropriate for his or her class. **Answer keys** are located directly after the **reproducible student materials** throughout the unit. The student materials may be reproduced for use in the teacher's classroom without copyright infringement. No other portion of this unit may be reproduced without the written consent of Teacher's Pet Publications, Inc.

UNIT OBJECTIVES *Medea*

1. Students will gain an understanding of the conventions of Greek drama and understand the ways Euripides uses these conventions.

2. Students will be able to explain what the *deus ex machina* is and why Euripides employs it in *Medea*.

3. Students will be able to explain how Euripides examines Medea's place as both a woman and a foreigner in the society of Corinth.

4. Students will be able to explain why Medea is both a sympathetic and unsympathetic character.

5. Students will be able to explain the role of the Chorus in Greek drama and in *Medea*.

6. Students will be given the opportunity to practice reading aloud and silently to improve their skills in each area.

7. Students will make connections with the material in the text and apply the lessons learned to their lives.

8. Students will answer questions to demonstrate their knowledge and understanding of the main events and characters as they relate to the author's theme development.

9. Students will demonstrate their understanding of the text on four levels: factual, interpretive, critical, and personal.

10. Students will enrich their vocabularies and improve their understanding of the play through the vocabulary lessons prepared for use in conjunction with the play.

11. Students will read aloud, report, and participate in large and small group discussions to improve their public speaking and personal interaction skills.

12. The writing assignments in this unit are designed for several purposes:

    a. to check and increase students' reading comprehension,

    b. to make students think about the ideas presented by the play,

    c. to encourage logical thinking,

    d. to provide an opportunity to practice good grammar and improve students' use of the English language,

    e. to encourage students' creativity.

READING ASSIGNMENTS *Medea*

Date Assigned	Assignment	Completion Date
	Reading Assignment 1 Prologue and Parodos	
	Reading Assignment 2 First Episode and Stasimon	
	Reading Assignment 3 Second Episode and Stasimon	
	Reading Assignment 4 Third Episode and Stasimon	
	Reading Assignment 5 Fourth Episode and Stasimon	
	Reading Assignment 6 Fifth Episode and Stasimon	
	Reading Assignment 7 Exodos	

UNIT OUTLINE *Medea*

1	2	3	4	5
Introduction Historical Background	Background Day 2 PV Prologue and Parodos R Prologue and Parodos for homework	Read Prologue and Parodos aloud Class discussion about moderation PV First Episode and Stasimon R First Episode and Stasimon for homework	Read First Episode and Stasimon aloud Discussion about Medea and Creon PV Second Episode and Stasimon R Second Episode and Stasimon for homework	Read Second Episode and Stasimon aloud Analyze relationship between Jason and Medea PV Third Episode and Stasimon R Third Episode and Stasimon for homework
6	7	8	9	10
Read Third Episode and Stasimon aloud Consider the Aegeus Episode PV Fourth Episode and Stasimon R Fourth Episode and Stasimon for homework	Read Fourth Episode and Stasimon aloud Relationship Timeline PV Fifth Episode and Stasimon R Fifth Episode and Stasimon for homework	Read Fifth Episode and Stasimon aloud Dramatic Irony PV Exodus R Exodus for homework	Read Exodus aloud Film Versions Tragic Odes	Theme Reports
11	12	13	14	15
Theme Reports Day 2 Work on Greek History Assignment	Writing Assignment 1	Making *Medea*	*Medea* Film Review	Writing Assignment 2
16	17	18	19	20
Extra Discussion Questions	Greek History Reports	Vocabulary Review	Unit Review	Unit Test Writing Assignment 3

Key: P = Preview Study Questions   V = Vocabulary Work   R = Read

STUDY GUIDE QUESTIONS

STUDY GUIDE QUESTIONS *Medea*

Reading Assignment 1
Prologue and Parodos
1. Where did Medea come from originally?
2. Where does the play take place?
3. What was the name of Jason's ship?
4. What happened to Pelias, and who was responsible for it?
5. According to the Nurse, why is Medea miserable?
6. What bad news does the Tutor bring to the Nurse?
7. What fear does the Nurse express?
8. What does the Nurse say about powerful people?
9. What kind of life does the Nurse want for herself?
10. Does Medea seem to be living the life of moderation that the Nurse favors?
11. What clue do we get from Medea herself about her capacity to commit violent acts?
12. To whom does Medea pray? Why is this significant?

Reading Assignment 2
First Episode and Stasimon
1. What does Medea blame for her unhappiness?
2. According to Medea, what problems do women face?
3. Besides the problems of women, what trouble does Medea mention?
4. What promise does Medea extract from the Chorus?
5. Describe Creon's manner of speaking. Is he direct or indirect?
6. What is Creon afraid of?
7. What does Medea say about cleverness?
8. What does Medea promise Creon?
9. What does Medea do to try to persuade Creon to let her stay?
10. Why does Creon allow Medea to stay in the country for one day?
11. What potential problem does Medea see in murdering her enemies directly?
12. What will determine how Medea carries out the murder?
13. What does the Chorus say about men and women?

Reading Assignment 3
Second Episode and Stasimon
1. According to Jason, why has he come to see Medea before she leaves?
2. What are some of the things Medea has done for Jason?
3. What are some ways in which Medea has benefited from marrying Jason, according to him?
4. Explain Jason's rationale for his poor treatment of Medea.
5. What kind of love is best, according to the Chorus?

6. What topic does the second part of the stasimon address?

Reading Assignment 4
Third Episode and Stasimon
1. What problem did Aegeus ask the oracle about, and what response did he get?
2. What promise does Medea extract from Aegeus?
3. What plan does Medea come up with to kill the princess?
4. How does the Chorus respond to Medea's plan?
5. How does the Chorus describe Athens?
6. How will Athens treat Medea, according to the Chorus?

Reading Assignment 5
Fourth Episode and Stasimon
1. What reason does Medea give Jason for her tears? What is the actual reason?
2. Who takes the gifts to the princess?
3. Why does Jason initially refuse the gifts? How does Medea convince him to accept them?
4. According to the Chorus, why is the delivery of the gifts the point of no return?

Reading Assignment 6
Fifth Episode and Stasimon
1. What emotions does Medea express to the children after they return from the palace?
2. What is the first thing the Messenger urges Medea to do?
3. How does Creon die?
4. What does the Chorus consider doing, and what is the reaction from inside the house?

Reading Assignment 7
Exodos
1. Where is Medea when Jason last sees her?
2. What does Jason beg of Medea? What is her reply?

STUDY GUIDE QUESTIONS ANSWER KEY *Medea*

Reading Assignment 1
Prologue and Parodos

1. Where did Medea come from originally?
   Colchis

2. Where does the play take place?
   Corinth

3. What was the name of Jason's ship?
   The Argo

4. What happened to Pelias, and who was responsible for it?
   Medea tricked Pelias' daughters into killing him.

5. According to the Nurse, why is Medea miserable?
   Jason, Medea's husband, has abandoned her to marry the daughter of Creon, the king of Corinth.

6. What bad news does the Tutor bring to the Nurse?
   He has heard a rumor that Medea and her children will be exiled from Corinth.

7. What fear does the Nurse express?
   She fears that Medea will do something to harm the children.

8. What does the Nurse say about powerful people?
   The Nurse says that power is bad for human beings; when powerful people get angry, they do a lot of damage. She prefers a life of moderation.

9. What kind of life does the Nurse want for herself?
   She wants a simple life. She fears that too much of anything will bring disaster.

10. Does Medea seem to be living the life of moderation that the Nurse favors?
    No. The Chorus warns her not to "pine excessively." She seems to other people to be too emotional.

11. What clue do we get from Medea herself about her capacity to commit violent acts?
    Medea killed her own brother to get away from her father, so she seems to be capable of anything.

12. To whom does Medea pray? Why is this significant?
    Medea prays to Zeus and Themis. Zeus is king of the gods, and Themis is the goddess of oaths. These are not trivial prayers—Medea is calling upon two powerful deities.

Reading Assignment 2
First Episode and Stasimon

1. What does Medea blame for her unhappiness?
   Medea says that her behavior is not proper for a foreigner or native citizen, but she can't help herself; the situation is too upsetting.

2. According to Medea, what problems do women face?
   Women have to buy marriage with dowries. Once they are married, they give up all power to their husbands. Society forces women to stay within their marriages whether or not they are happy. Women have no way of knowing whether they will be happy before they get married, and no one teaches them how to deal with men. Furthermore, marriage can endanger their lives; they may die in childbirth, or their husbands may be violent.

3. Besides the problems of women, what trouble does Medea mention?
   Medea is a foreigner; she has no friends or family to whom she can escape.
4. What promise does Medea extract from the Chorus?
   The Chorus will keep silent about Medea's plans for revenge against Jason.
5. Describe Creon's manner of speaking. Is he direct or indirect?
   Creon is direct; he gets right to the point. He tells Medea that she has to leave immediately.
6. What is Creon afraid of?
   Creon fears that Medea will harm him, his daughter, or Jason.
7. What does Medea say about cleverness?
   Cleverness never benefits anyone—a clever person is useless among stupid people, and suspect among others.
8. What does Medea promise Creon?
   Medea promises she will not injure him.
9. What does Medea do to try to persuade Creon to let her stay?
   She pleads with him and embraces his knees.
10. Why does Creon allow Medea to stay in the country for one day?
    He reasons that one day is not long enough for her to do anything terrible.
11. What potential problem does Medea see in murdering her enemies directly?
    She might get caught in the act and stopped. Everyone would laugh at her.
12. What will determine how Medea carries out the murder?
    If Medea has somewhere to run, she will be stealthy about the murder, but if she does not, she will kill herself in the act.
13. What does the Chorus say about men and women?
    The Chorus says that women are traditionally thought of as tricky and unfaithful, but men are the real cheaters.

Reading Assignment 3
Second Episode and Stasimon
1. According to Jason, why has he come to see Medea before she leaves?
   Jason says that he is trying to make sure that Medea and the children are provided for.
2. What are some of the things Medea has done for Jason?
   Medea helped Jason kill the dragon that was guarding the Golden Fleece, she betrayed her father in order to marry Jason, and she had Pelias brutally murdered.
3. What are some ways in which Medea has benefited from marrying Jason, according to him?
   Jason says that Medea gets to live in a civilized place and learn how to use laws. Living in Greece also means that she will be remembered rather than forgotten.
4. Explain Jason's rationale for his poor treatment of Medea.
   Jason says that marrying the princess will benefit everyone; he can join the two families so that they will all be well off.
5. What kind of love is best, according to the Chorus?
   The Chorus praises love in moderation. Excessive love, like Medea's, is dangerous.
6. What topic does the second part of the stasimon address?
   The Chorus discusses exile from one's native land, calling it the most terrible thing a person can go through.

Reading Assignment 4
Third Episode and Stasimon
1. What problem did Aegeus ask the oracle about, and what response did he get?
   Aegeus wants to have a child. The oracle told him not to "loosen the wineskin's protruding foot" before he got home (i.e., not to have intercourse before returning home).
2. What promise does Medea extract from Aegeus?
   Medea says she will give Aegeus drugs that will help him have children if he will promise to take her in after she flees Corinth.
3. What plan does Medea come up with to kill the princess?
   She will tell Jason she has made peace with his new marriage and then have her sons deliver to the princess a dress and crown laced with poison. The princess will die when she wears these items.
4. How does the Chorus respond to Medea's plan?
   The Chorus is horrified and begs Medea to reconsider her decision.
5. How does the Chorus describe Athens?
   Athens is a blessed, holy place, where the people enjoy wisdom and harmony.
6. How will Athens treat Medea, according to the Chorus?
   The Chorus cannot fathom how a place as holy as Athens can take in someone who has done something as unholy as killing her own children.

Reading Assignment 5
Fourth Episode and Stasimon
1. What reason does Medea give Jason for her tears? What is the actual reason?
   Medea says that women are naturally given to crying. She also says that she is worried about the children's future. In reality, Medea is crying because she knows she is going to kill them.
2. Who takes the gifts to the princess?
   Medea sends the children to give her the gifts.
3. Why does Jason initially refuse the gifts? How does Medea convince him to accept them?
   Jason says that the princess does not need any more dresses. Medea tells him that the dresses may play a part in getting the children's exile repealed.
4. According to the Chorus, why is the delivery of the gifts the point of no return?
   Knowing Medea's character and intention, the Chorus is aware that the delivery of gifts to the princess seals the fate of the children.

Reading Assignment 6
Fifth Episode and Stasimon
1. What emotions does Medea express to the children after they return from the palace?
   Medea wavers between sadness that she will never see them again and resolution to follow through with her plan to kill them.
2. What is the first thing the Messenger urges Medea to do?
   He tells Medea to run away immediately.
3. How does Creon die?
   When Creon embraces his dead daughter, the dress clings to him, and the poison rubs off on him.

4. What does the Chorus consider doing, and what is the reaction from inside the house?
   The Chorus thinks of intervening and stopping the murder. One of the children begs for this to happen, but then the Chorus decides against it.

Reading Assignment 7
Exodos
1. Where is Medea when Jason last sees her?
   She is flying over Jason's head in a chariot pulled by dragons.
2. What does Jason beg of Medea? What is her reply?
   He begs to be allowed to bury his children. Medea refuses; she tells him she will bury them herself.

MULTIPLE CHOICE STUDY/QUIZ QUESTIONS
Medea

Reading Assignment 1
Prologue and Parodos

1. Where did Medea come from originally?

    A. Athens

    B. Sparta

    C. Corinth

    D. Colchis

2. Where does the play take place?

    A. Athens

    B. Pelias

    C. Corinth

    D. Colchis

3. What was the name of Jason's ship?

    A. the *Mighty Jason*

    B. the *Bounty*

    C. the *Golden Fleece*

    D. the *Argo*

4. What happened to Pelias, and who was responsible for it?

    A. Jason killed him in battle.

    B. Medea poisoned him.

    C. He died of natural causes; no one was responsible.

    D. Medea tricked Pelias' daughters into killing him.

5. According to the Nurse, why is Medea miserable?

    A. Medea and Jason have been forbidden to see each other.

    B. Creon, Jason's uncle, has demanded that Medea marry him.

    C. Medea is sorry about what happened to Pelias.

    D. Jason abandoned her to marry the daughter of the king of Corinth.

6. What fear does the Nurse express?

    A. She fears that she will be exiled from Corinth.

    B. She fears that the children will become seriously ill.

    C. She fears that Medea will do something to harm the children.

    D. She fears that the gods will punish Medea.

7. What bad news does the Tutor bring to the nurse?
   A. Jason has decided to marry Creon's daughter.
   B. Medea and her children have been exiled from Corinth.
   C. Creon has decided that the children no longer need a nurse.
   D. Medea is unhappy in Corinth and wants to go home.

8. What does the Nurse say about power?
   A. Power is good for men, but not for women.
   B. People abuse power, but should still have it.
   C. People like power and should have it.
   D. Power is dangerous and can cause harm.

9. What kind of life does the Nurse want to lead?
   A. a simple, moderate life
   B. a holy, quiet life
   C. a legendary but tragic life
   D. a brief, exciting life

10. To whom does Medea pray?
    A. Medusa and Pelion
    B. Zeus and Themis
    C. Pegasus and Aegeus
    D. Hades and Jason

Reading Assignment 2
First Episode and Stasimon

1. What does Medea emphasize in her description of the lives of women?
    A. boredom
    B. cost
    C. difficulty
    D. fulfillment

2. What sets Medea apart in Corinthian society?
    A. Medea has two children; most women have more.
    B. Jason, Medea's husband, is not from Greece, but from Asia Minor.
    C. Medea is a foreigner; she has no friends or family to support her.
    D. Medea is much older than most of the people around her.

3. What promise does Medea extract from the Chorus?
    A. The Chorus will keep silent about Medea's plans for revenge against Jason.
    B. The Chorus will help Medea get out of Corinth.
    C. The Chorus will get even with Jason for abandoning Medea.
    D. The Chorus will take care of Medea's children.

4. Which word best describes Creon?
    A. direct
    B. gullible
    C. kind
    D. indecisive

5. Why does Creon exile Medea?
    A. He fears that she will harm him or his family.
    B. He does not like Jason.
    C. He has been told to do so by the oracle.
    D. He thinks she is someone else.

6. What does Medea promise Creon?
    A. that she will not injure him
    B. that she will attend Jason's wedding
    C. that she will visit the oracle
    D. that her children will avenge her

7. What does Medea do to try to persuade Creon to let her stay?
    A. She prays to Zeus.
    B. She gives him a gold crown.
    C. She offers him her children.
    D. She embraces Creon's knees.

8. Why does Creon allow Medea to stay in the country for one day?
    A. He needs her to make a potion for him.
    B. He wants to get back at his daughter for marrying Jason.
    C. He will be leaving Corinth in one day.
    D. He reasons that Medea cannot do anything terrible in one day.

9. What does Medea fear that her enemies might do if she tries to murder them directly?
    A. overpower and kill her
    B. take revenge on her children and Jason
    C. call down the gods' punishment upon her
    D. stop her in the act, making her a laughingstock

10. On what will Medea's method of killing her enemies depend?
    A. whether she has a place to escape to
    B. how Creon and Jason treat her
    C. how much money she has
    D. the answer she gets from the gods

11. According to the Chorus, who is most unfaithful?
    A. women
    B. Greeks
    C. men
    D. children

Reading Assignment 3
Second Episode and Stasimon

1. According to Jason, why has he come to see Medea before she leaves?
    A. He needs Medea's advice about Creon.
    B. He is desperate for Medea to stay in Corinth.
    C. He wants to make sure that Medea and the children are provided for.
    D. He is leaving Corinth, and he may never see the children again.

2. Which of the following is NOT something Medea did for Jason, according to the speech she makes?
    A. She helped Jason kill the dragon that was guarding the Golden Fleece.
    B. She allowed Jason to divorce her and marry Creon's daughter.
    C. She had Pelias brutally murdered.
    D. She betrayed her father in order to marry Jason.

3. How has Medea benefited from being married to Jason, according to him?
    A. She has lived in a civilized place and learned how to use laws.
    B. She has a room in the palace, and she is best friends with the princess.
    C. She has been given citizenship and the right to vote.
    D. She has been able to share her culture with the people of Corinth.

4. What does Jason say about his marriage to the princess?
    A. It will not make a difference to Medea or Creon.
    B. It will be bad for Medea, but it is nonetheless the right thing to do.
    C. It will benefit Medea and Jason; they can take Creon's money and flee.
    D. It will benefit everyone; joining his two families will make them all well off.

5. Which is best, according to the Chorus?
    A. passion
    B. exile
    C. moderation
    D. mercy

Reading Assignment 4
Third Episode and Stasimon

1. What problem did Aegeus ask the oracle about?
    A. He cannot sleep.
    B. He is depressed.
    C. He cannot have children.
    D. He wants a divorce.

2. What does Medea make Aegeus promise to do?
    A. leave her all his money
    B. give her safe harbor
    C. adopt her children
    D. talk to Creon for her

3. What will Medea use to kill the princess?
    A. a poisoned dress
    B. a bewitched cup of wine
    C. a knife
    D. a noose

4. Which word best describes the Chorus' response to Medea's plan?
    A. confused
    B. indifferent
    C. horrified
    D. thrilled

Reading Assignment 5
Fourth Episode and Stasimon

1. What reason does Medea give Jason for her tears?
    A. She is very angry with him.
    B. She has not been feeling well lately.
    C. She regrets giving anything to the princess.
    D. She is a woman, and, therefore, naturally sensitive.

2. Who takes the gifts in to the princess?
    A. Jason
    B. children
    C. Creon
    D. Medea

3. How does Medea convince Jason to accept the gifts?
    A. She points out that they are as good as anything made by the Greeks.
    B. She tells him that they may help get the children's exile repealed.
    C. She emphasizes the trouble she took to prepare them.
    D. She says that if he loves her, he will accept them.

Reading Assignment 6
Fifth Episode and Stasimon

1. What is the first thing the Messenger urges Medea to do?
    A. run away immediately
    B. apologize to the princess
    C. save the children
    D. hide in the palace

2. How does Creon die?
    A. Upon seeing his dead daughter, he jumps into the sea and drowns.
    B. When he embraces his dead daughter, the dress clings to him, and the poison kills him.
    C. He gets into a fight with Jason and is fatally stabbed.
    D. The gods strike him down in vengeance for his actions toward Medea.

3. What happens as Medea is murdering the children?
    A. Strange music is heard in the palace.
    B. Medea laughs and cries at the same time.
    C. Jason runs in and intervenes.
    D. The Chorus and the children briefly converse.

Reading Assignment 7
Exodos

1. Where is Medea when Jason last sees her?
    A. on a boat headed for Athens
    B. in front of Creon's throne
    C. at the funeral of her children
    D. in a chariot pulled by dragons

2. What does Jason beg Medea to do?
    A. kill him also
    B. allow him to bury his children
    C. apologize to the people of Corinth
    D. stay married to him

3. Medea responds to Jason's request by
    A. refusing.
    B. agreeing.
    C. disappearing.
    D. ignoring him.

ANSWER KEY: STUDY QUESTIONS *Medea*

	1	2	3	4	5	6	7
1	D	C	C	C	D	A	D
2	C	C	B	B	B	B	B
3	D	A	A	A	B	D	A
4	D	A	D	C			
5	D	A	C				
6	C	A					
7	B	D					
8	D	D					
9	A	D					
10	B	A					
11		C					

VOCABULARY WORKSHEETS

VOCABULARY READING ASSIGNMENT 1 *Medea*

Part I: Using Prior Knowledge and Contextual Clues

Below are the sentences in which the vocabulary words appear in the text. Read the sentence. Use any clues you can find in the sentence combined with your prior knowledge, and write what you think the underlined words mean on the lines provided.

1. ...when she hears her friend <u>rebuke</u> her,
   she listens like a rock or the sea's wave...

   _____

2. Nurse: I won't wish him death, for he's still my master,
       but he has proven bad to his friends.

   Tutor: What <u>mortal</u> isn't? Do you learn this now?
       Every single person loves himself more than his fellow man, if a father
       does not love his children because of his bed.

   _____

3. ...forced to live
   in this land of Corinth with her husband
   and children, an <u>exile</u> who pleased the citizens
   of her new home...

   _____

4. Don't go near her, but watch out
   for her fierce heart and the hateful nature
   of her <u>contumacious</u> mind.

   _____

5. I have suffered, oh, dreadfully
   have I suffered things
   worthy of <u>lamentation</u>.

   _____

6. First of all, the very idea of <u>moderation</u>
   wins first prize in speaking, and in action,
   is far the best way for mortals, but excessive power
   can produce no proper return for human beings...

   _____

Medea Vocabulary Worksheet Reading Assignment 1 Continued

Part II: Determining the Meaning -- Match the vocabulary words to their dictionary definitions.

____ 1. REBUKE   A. mourning

____ 2. MORTAL   B. a human

____ 3. EXILE   C. balance

____ 4. CONTUMACIOUS   D. to criticize

____ 5. LAMENTATION   E. an outcast

____ 6. MODERATION   F. rebellious

VOCABULARY READING ASSIGNMENT 2 *Medea*

Part I: Using Prior Knowledge and Contextual Clues

Below are the sentences in which the vocabulary words appear in the text. Read the sentence. Use any clues you can find in the sentence combined with your prior knowledge, and write what you think the underlined words mean on the lines provided.

1. Women of Corinth, I came out of the house
   so that you would not <u>reproach</u> me.

   _____

2. A foreigner,
   especially, ought to make <u>concessions</u>
   to the city...

   _____

3. ...I have been outraged by my husband
   and am alone, without city, carried off
   from a <u>barbarian</u> land...

   _____

4. My enemies have opened my sails to the wind,
   and there is no <u>haven</u> to escape ruin.

   _____

5. ...when the city thinks you superior
   to those who seem to have <u>abstruse</u> knowledge,
   you will annoy them.

   _____

6. I don't have a <u>dictatorial</u> nature,
   and I've often lost by being considerate.

   _____

7. There's just one little thing <u>hindering</u> me—
   if I am caught entering the house, scheming,
   I will die and become a source of laughter
   for my enemies.

   _____

8. You must not <u>incur</u> mockery through these Corinthian marriages of Jason's...

   _____

9. ...Phoebus, leader of songs, did not give
   to my <u>comprehension</u> the inspired song
   of the lyre...

   _____

10. Phoebus, leader of songs, did not give to my comprehension the inspired song of the <u>lyre</u>...

_____

Part II: Determining the Meaning -- Match the vocabulary words to their dictionary definitions.

____ 1. REPROACH   A. to cause; invite

____ 2. CONCESSIONS   B. stopping

____ 3. BARBARIAN   C. a stringed instrument

____ 4. HAVEN   D. hard to understand

____ 5. ABSTRUSE   E. to scold

____ 6. DICTATORIAL   F. understanding

____ 7. HINDERING   G. bossy

____ 8. INCUR   H. a safe place

____ 9. COMPREHENSION   I. savage

____ 10. LYRE   J. allowances

VOCABULARY READING ASSIGNMENT 3 *Medea*

Part I: Using Prior Knowledge and Contextual Clues

Below are the sentences in which the vocabulary words appear in the text. Read the sentence. Use any clues you can find in the sentence combined with your prior knowledge, and write what you think the underlined words mean on the lines provided.

1. You could have remained in this land and house,
   if you had meekly obeyed the ruler's will;
   but, because of <u>rash</u> words, you are thrown out of the country.

   _____

2. You entirely vile man—that's the greatest insult
   my tongue can <u>wield</u> against your cowardice...

   _____

3. Come, I'll share with you as if you were my friend. (Thinking to get something good from you?) No, but being questioned, you'll be proven <u>base</u>.

   _____

4. I will go into exile from this,
   <u>bereft</u> of friends, alone with only my children.

   _____

Medea Vocabulary Worksheet Reading Assignment 3 Continued

Part II: Determining the Meaning -- Match the vocabulary words to their dictionary definitions.

____ 1. RASH   A. careless; foolish

____ 2. WIELD   B. low; evil

____ 3. BASE   C. to use

____ 4. BEREFT   D. without, lacking

VOCABULARY READING ASSIGNMENT 4 *Medea*

Part I: Using Prior Knowledge and Contextual Clues

Below are the sentences in which the vocabulary words appear in the text. Read the sentence. Use any clues you can find in the sentence combined with your prior knowledge, and write what you think the underlined words mean on the lines provided.

1. Medea: Do you have a wife, or is your bed empty?

    Aegeus: I do not lack a <u>nuptial</u> couch.

    _____

2. Please, I beseech you by your beard and your knees!
   I am your <u>suppliant</u>.

    _____

3. Medea: ...What will you suffer if you break the oath?

    Aegeus: That which comes to <u>impious</u> mortals.

    _____

4. I can tack my sails
   on him and steer for the city and
   <u>bastion</u> of Athena.

    _____

5. When he comes,
   I will speak soothing words to him, how I think
   he's right, he made a good marriage with the king—
   the marriage he has now that he's betrayed us—
   that it's <u>prudent</u>, he knew what he was doing.

    _____

6. ...and her hair
   is crowned with a fragrant <u>garland</u> of flowers...

    _____

7. ...how will you keep your <u>resolve</u>
   to kill them?

    _____

Medea Vocabulary Worksheet Reading Assignment 4 Continued

Part II: Determining the Meaning -- Match the vocabulary words to their dictionary definitions.

____ 1.   NUPTIAL   A. related to marriage

____ 2.   SUPPLIANT   B. lacking respect for religion

____ 3.   IMPIOUS   C. determination

____ 4.   BASTION   D. someone who pleads

____ 5.   PRUDENT   E. a strong place

____ 6.   GARLAND   F. sensible

____ 7.   RESOLVE   G. a wreath

VOCABULARY READING ASSIGNMENT 5 *Medea*

Part I: Using Prior Knowledge and Contextual Clues

Below are the sentences in which the vocabulary words appear in the text. Read the sentence. Use any clues you can find in the sentence combined with your prior knowledge, and write what you think the underlined words mean on the lines provided.

1. Then ask your wife to entreat her father
   not to expel the children from the country.

   _____

2. She will be happy not in one way only,
   but ten thousand, finding a peerless husband...

   _____

3. Take it for her dowry, boys,
   in your hands, and give it to the princess,
   the blessed bride; she will not despise these gifts.

   _____

4. ...because of a bridal bed that your husband
   left behind along with you
   unlawfully to live with another consort.

   _____

5. She'll wear her bridal garb among the dead.

   _____

Medea Vocabulary Worksheet Reading Assignment 5 Continued

Part II: Determining the Meaning -- Match the vocabulary words to their dictionary definitions.

____ 1.   ENTREAT   A. a mate, especially one outside of marriage

____ 2.   PEERLESS   B. to ask

____ 3.   DOWRY   C. a bridal price

____ 4.   CONSORT   D. clothing

____ 5.   GARB   E. unmatched

VOCABULARY READING ASSIGNMENT 6 *Medea*

Part I: Using Prior Knowledge and Contextual Clues

Below are the sentences in which the vocabulary words appear in the text. Read the sentence. Use any clues you can find in the sentence combined with your prior knowledge, and write what you think the underlined words mean on the lines provided.

1. A most beautiful tale you've told, and I will count
   you as a friend and <u>benefactor</u> forever!

   _____

2. …She cast down her eyes and turned away her white cheek, in disgust at the children's entrance. But your husband
   took away the young lady's anger and <u>bile</u>…

   _____

3. …her <u>complexion</u> altered, she went back slantwise,
   her limbs shaking…she could see white foam coming from her mouth and the girl's
   eyes twisting in their sockets, the blood gone from her face.

   _____

4. In vain the labor of children is lost,
   in vain, indeed, you bore that dear race,
   O you who left the dark-blue rock of the
   Symplegades, that most <u>inhospitable</u> passage.

   _____

5. Wretched woman, why does heart-oppressing <u>wrath</u>
   fall on you, and why does terrible
   murder answer murder?

   _____

6. She fell, poor woman, into the sea, in an
   impious murder of her children,
   stepping too far on the <u>promontory</u>,
   and she perished, dying with her two sons.

   _____

Medea Vocabulary Worksheet Reading Assignment 6 Continued

Part II: Determining the Meaning -- Match the vocabulary words to their dictionary definitions.

____ 1. BENEFACTOR   A. coloring

____ 2. BILE   B. a helper

____ 3. COMPLEXION   C. hatred

____ 4. INHOSPITABLE   D. anger

____ 5. WRATH   E. a cliff

____ 6. PROMONTORY   F. unfriendly

VOCABULARY READING ASSIGNMENT 7 *Medea*

Part I: Using Prior Knowledge and Contextual Clues

Below are the sentences in which the vocabulary words appear in the text. Read the sentence. Use any clues you can find in the sentence combined with your prior knowledge, and write what you think the underlined words mean on the lines provided.

1. ...I enjoin upon this
   land of Sisyphus a solemn festival...

   _____

2. ...I enjoin upon this
   land of Sisyphus a solemn festival
   and rites for all time in expiation
   of this impious murder.

   _____

3. ...you killed my children and then prevented me
   from touching them and burying their corpses,
   whom I would never have sired
   to see them dead by your hands.

   _____

Medea Vocabulary Worksheet Reading Assignment 7 Continued

Part II: Determining the Meaning -- Match the vocabulary words to their dictionary definitions.

____ 1. ENJOIN   A. fathered

____ 2. EXPIATION   B. to command; order

____ 3. SIRED   C. repayment for a wrong

VOCABULARY ANSWER KEY - *Medea*

	1	2	3	4	5	6	7
1	D	E	A	A	B	B	B
2	B	J	C	D	E	C	C
3	E	I	B	B	C	A	A
4	F	H	D	E	A	F	
5	A	D		F	D	D	
6	C	G		G		E	
7		B		C			
8		A					
9		F					
10		C					

DAILY LESSONS

LESSON ONE

<u>Objectives</u>
1. To introduce the *Medea* unit
2. To distribute books and other related materials
3. To learn about Greek theater

<u>Activity #1</u>
Ask students what they know about ancient Greek theater. Have they ever seen the masks used in Greek tragedy and comedy? Have they ever heard of a Greek Chorus? Have each student fill out the KWL paper for Greek tragedy.

<u>Activity #2</u>
Distribute the materials students will use in this unit. Explain in detail how students are to use these materials.

<u>Study Guides</u> Students should preview the study guide questions before each reading assignment to get a feeling for what events and ideas are important in that section. After reading the section, students will (as a class or individually) answer the questions to review the important events and ideas from that section of the play. Students should keep the study guides as study materials for the unit test.

<u>Reading Assignment Sheet</u> You need to fill in the reading assignment sheet to let students know when their reading has to be completed. You can either write the assignment sheet on a side blackboard or bulletin board and leave it there for students to see each day, or you can make copies for each student to have. In either case, you should advise students to become very familiar with the reading assignments so they know what is expected of them.

<u>Extra Activities Center</u> The resource materials portion of this unit contains crossword and word search puzzles. Make an extra activities center in your room where you will keep these materials for students to use. (Keep several copies of the puzzles on hand.) Explain to students that these materials are available for students to use when they finish reading assignments or other class work early.

<u>Nonfiction Assignment Sheet</u> Explain to students that they each are to read at least one nonfiction piece at some time during the unit. Students will fill out a nonfiction assignment sheet after completing the reading to help you evaluate their reading experiences and to help them think about and evaluate their own reading experiences.

<u>Greek History Research Sheet</u> Explain to students that they are to briefly explain each term on the sheet as they work through the unit. They can do research online or in the library.

<u>Books</u> Each school has its own rules and regulations regarding student use of school books. Advise students of the procedures that are normal for your school.

<u>Activity #3</u>

Label the picture of the Greek theater. If something is not in the picture, draw it in, and label it.

- A. Chorus—the group of actors who comment on the action
- B. choragos—the leader of the Chorus
- C. deus ex machina—"god from the machine"—a device that neatly solves the problems of the plot at the end of the play

D. ekkyklema—a wheeled cart on which dead bodies are usually brought out
E. orchestra—the area in front of the stage where the Chorus dances
F. theatron—the area from which the spectators watch the action
G. skene—the building behind the stage through which actors enter and exit
H. proskenion—the area in front of the skene where the action takes place

KWL CHART

Before reading, think about what you already know about Greek theater, Euripides, and the Medea story. Write the information in the K column. Think about what you would like to find out from reading the play. Write your questions in the W column. After you have read the play, use the L column to write the answers to your questions from the W column, and anything else you remember from the play.

K	W	L
What I Know	**What I Want to Find Out**	**What I Learned**

GREEK HISTORY WORKSHEET
(To be completed as you work through the unit)

Name: _____   **Date:** _____

Complete this assignment as you work through the unit. Write a brief description of the following items as they relate to 5th century Greece:

Socrates -

Plato -

Aeschylus -

Sophocles -

Pericles -

Athens -

Persian War -

Sparta -

Marathon -

Aristophanes -

Peloponnesian War -

Thucydides -

Great Dionysia -

NONFICTION ASSIGNMENT SHEET
(To be completed after reading the required nonfiction article)

Name: _____ Date: _____

Title of Nonfiction Read: _____

Author: _____ Date Published: _____

I. Factual Summary
Write a short summary of the work you read.

II. Vocabulary
1. Which vocabulary words were difficult to understand to some degree?

2. How did you resolve your lack of understanding of these words?

III. Interpretation
What was the main point the author wanted you to get from reading his or her work?

IV. Criticism
1. Which points did you agree with or find easy to accept? Why?

2. Which points did you disagree with or find difficult to believe? Why?

V. Personal Response
What do you think about this work? OR How does this work influence your ideas?

LESSON TWO

Objectives
1. To learn the mythology behind *Medea*
2. To go over the parts of a Greek play
3. To preview the study questions for the Prologue and Parodos
4. To familiarize students with the vocabulary for the Prologue and Parodos

Activity #1
In this activity, students will put on brief skits to make the mythological background of *Medea* clear.

Divide the class into six groups. Hand out a copy of the "Mythological Background" worksheet to each group.

Each group will cover one of the following sections of the story:

1) Pelius locks up Aeson and hears the prophecy about the man wearing one sandal; Jason returns.

2) The story of the Golden Fleece

3) Jason has the *Argo* built and sets off for Colchis.

4) Jason meets Medea, and she helps him get back the Golden Fleece.

5) Jason and Medea flee Colchis.

6) Medea kills Pelias.

Each group will put on a one-minute skit to explain its section of the story to the rest of the class.

Activity #2
Go over the main parts of a Greek play. Explain that Greek plays follow a formal structure, with *episodes* (periods of action) followed by *choral odes*, or *stasimons*. Each ode is divided into two or three parts (strophe, antistrophe, and sometimes epode).

The play begins with a *prologue* (section before the chorus enters); this is followed by a *parodos* (the Chorus' opening song). A *kommos* is a lament shared by the chorus and main character.

After reviewing this information, have the students complete the "Play Terms in Action" Worksheet by filling in the blanks.

Activity #3
Review the study questions and vocabulary for the Prologue and Parodos orally together in class. Tell students that they should read the Prologue and Parodos prior to the next class period. Give them the remainder of this class (if time remains) to complete this assignment.

MYTHOLOGICAL BACKGROUND

Pelias is the half-brother of Aeson, who is the father of Jason. He rules over Iolcus in Thessaly. Pelias wants to be ruler of Thessaly, so he locks up Aeson in a dungeon. While in the dungeon, Aeson marries and has children, one of whom is Jason. Jason is sent away. Meanwhile, Pelias hears a prophecy that he will be overthrown by a man wearing one sandal.

When Jason comes of age, he goes back to Iolcus. On the way, he loses a shoe in the river. Pelias realizes who Jason is and tries to get rid of him by sending him on a quest for the Golden Fleece.

The Golden Fleece is the skin of a special ram that had carried Phrixus and Helle, two children of Athamas and Nephele, to the kingdom of Colchis. Helle fell off the ram in the strait between the Sea of Marmara and the Aegean Sea; this strait was named the *Hellespont* after her. (Now it's called the *Dardanelles.*) When Phrixus got to Colchis, he sacrificed the ram. King Aetes of Colchis put the fleece under guard of a dragon.

Jason sets off to get the fleece, but he needs a ship. He hires Argus to build him a huge ship, which he names the *Argo*. The fifty men who sail with Jason are known as the *Argonauts*. Jason's quest is difficult; like other Greek heroes, he has to overcome many obstacles before he actually gets to Colchis.

The Argonauts land on the island of Lemnos, which is populated only by women. (They have killed their husbands.) The inhabitants of Lemnos may be fierce, but they help the Argonauts.

On an island in the Black Sea, the Argonauts encounter Phineas (who is also mentioned in *Medea*). The gods have cursed him; evil half-bird, half-woman creatures called *harpies* swoop down and snatch his food every time he tries to eat. Jason and his Argonauts drive the harpies away. In return, Phineas tells them how to get past the *Symplegades* (rocks that clashed together in the *Bosphorus*, a passage between the Sea of Marmara and the Black Sea).

When Jason reaches Colchis, he gets help from Medea, the daughter of King Aetes, in recovering the Golden Fleece. Medea is a witch, so she is able to drug the dragon. In return for her help, Jason marries Medea.

As they are escaping from Colchis, Medea's father chases them. Medea kills her own brother and scatters the pieces of his body. King Aetes has to gather up all the pieces so that the body can be properly buried. As he stops to do this, Medea and Jason get away.

Back in Thessaly, Medea restores Jason's father, Aeson, to youth at Jason's request. She does this by cutting the old man's throat and pouring a special potion into his wounds. She tells the daughters of Pelias that she will do the same for their father, so they slice him into pieces. She then refuses to bring him back.

Jason and Medea flee to Corinth, where the play takes place.

PLAY TERMS IN ACTION

Review the following terms, then fill in each blank with the proper term:

1. ode — the song the Chorus sings after each episode
2. strophe — the first part of the ode
3. antistrophe — the second part of the ode
4. epode — the third part of the ode
5. kommos — a song shared by the Chorus and a main character
6. stasimon — the Greek term for ode; it takes place between dramatic episodes.
7. prologue — the part of the play before the Chorus enters
8. parodos — the first entrance of the chorus
9. episode — spoken lines; it takes place between odes.

Medea begins with a(n) _____ in which the Nurse explains why she is troubled. The Chorus then marches in for the _____, or opening song. The Chorus and Medea join together for a(n) _____. Following the first _____, there is a choral _____, or _____, which sums up the action that has taken place. In the _____ of the _____, the Chorus talks about how men and women are not equal; in the _____, it deals with Medea's plan. There is no unmatched stanza, or _____, in this section.

PLAY TERMS IN ACTION ANSWER KEY

Medea begins with a(n) prologue in which the Nurse explains why she is troubled. The Chorus then marches in for the parodos, or opening song. The Chorus and Medea join together for a(n) kommos. Following the first episode, there is a choral ode, or stasimon, which sums up the action that has taken place. In the strophe of the ode, the chorus talks about how men and women are not equal; in the antistrophe, it deals with Medea's plan. There is no unmatched stanza, or epode, in this section.

LESSON THREE

Objectives
1. To start to discuss the characters in the play
2. To read the Prologue and Parodos aloud
3. To evaluate students' oral reading
4. To discuss the idea of moderation in Greek thought and in *Medea*
5. To preview the study questions for the First Episode and Stasimon
6. To familiarize students with the vocabulary in the First Episode and Stasimon

Activity #1
As a lead-in to the reading of the play, have the students spend five minutes responding to one of the following journal prompts.

Briefly write about a time when someone betrayed you. What was the person's relationship to you? How close were you, and how much did you trust this person? Why did the person do what he or she did? How did you find out? How long did it take you to get over the betrayal?

OR

Write about a time when someone you know reacted in an extreme way in response to something. What prompted the reaction? Why did it seem extreme to you? How did you feel around this person? Did you say anything?

Activity #2
Nurse
Tutor
Medea
Chorus (several students)

Assign the parts listed above to some of the students in your class. Read up to the end of the Parodos (right before Medea's emergence from the house) orally.

NOTE: If you have not yet evaluated your students' oral reading for this marking period, this is an excellent chance to do so. An oral reading evaluation form is provided for your convenience following this lesson.

Activity #3
Divide the class into several small groups. Hand out copies of the Mystery Quote worksheet to each group. Allow about five minutes for the groups to work out the basic meaning of the passage.

Bring the class back together and ask for a volunteer or two to explain what the passage means. Then, tell the class that the quote is from an important Greek philosopher, Aristotle. Explain that ideas of balance, moderation, and self-control were very important in Greek philosophy; the temple of the Delphic Oracle (which is visited by a character later in the play) even had the inscription, "Meden Agan" ("Nothing in Excess").

Ask the class to consider the character of Medea (especially what the Nurse says about her) in light of this information. Encourage students to use specific examples from the text to support what they say.

Activity #4
Review the study questions and vocabulary for the First Episode and Stasimon orally together in class. Tell students that they should read the First Episode and Stasimon prior to the next class period. Give them the remainder of this class (if time remains) to complete this assignment.

Advise students to keep the following questions in mind as they read the First Episode and Stasimon:

—Why is Medea an outsider?

—What feelings about Medea have both the Chorus and the Nurse expressed?

ORAL READING EVALUATION FORM – *MEDEA*

Name: _____   Class: _____   Date: _____

SKILL	EXCELLENT	GOOD	AVERAGE	FAIR	POOR
Fluency	5	4	3	2	1
Clarity	5	4	3	2	1
Audibility	5	4	3	2	1
Pronunciation	5	4	3	2	1
_____	5	4	3	2	1
_____	5	4	3	2	1

Total _____   Grade _____

Comments:

_____

_____

_____

_____

_____

_____

_____

MYSTERY QUOTE

Read the following passage. Explain what it means in your own words.

"First, then, let us consider this, that it is the nature of such things to be destroyed by defect and excess, as we see in the case of strength and of health (for to gain light on things imperceptible we must use the evidence of sensible things); both excessive and defective exercise destroys the strength, and similarly drink or food which is above or below a certain amount destroys the health, while that which is proportionate both produces and increases and preserves it. So too is it, then, in the case of temperance and courage and the other virtues. For the man who flies from and fears everything and does not stand his ground against anything becomes a coward, and the man who fears nothing at all but goes to meet every danger becomes rash; and similarly the man who indulges in every pleasure and abstains from none becomes self-indulgent, while the man who shuns every pleasure, as boors do, becomes in a way insensible; temperance and courage, then, are destroyed by excess and defect, and preserved by the mean."

Meaning:

_____
_____
_____
_____
_____
_____
_____
_____
_____
_____
_____
_____

LESSON FOUR

Objectives
1. To review the Prologue and Parodos
2. To read the First Episode and Stasimon aloud
3. To analyze Medea's relationship with Creon and her position as a woman
4. To preview the study questions for the Second Episode and Stasimon
5. To familiarize students with the vocabulary for the Second Episode and Stasimon

Activity #1
As a class, briefly review the Prologue and Parodos: the Nurse gave some exposition, the Chorus made its first appearance, and we got our first glimpse of Medea's character, which is not marked by moderation.

Activity #2
Medea
Creon
Chorus (several students)

Assign the parts listed above to some of the students in your class. Read up to the end of the First Episode and Stasimon orally.

Activity #3
As a class, discuss the conversation between Medea and Creon. Lead the discussion by making two columns (on the board, smartboard, overhead, etc.) titled "Justified" and "Sympathetic." Decide whether Medea and Creon fit into each category using evidence from the text.

Activity #4
Review the study questions and vocabulary for the Second Episode and Stasimon orally together in class. Tell students that they should read the Second Episode and Stasimon prior to the next class period. Give them the remainder of this class (if time remains) to complete this assignment.

Ask students to remember Medea's relationship with Creon as they read her conversation with Jason.

LESSON FIVE

<u>Objectives</u>
1. To review the First Episode and Stasimon
2. To read the Second Episode and Stasimon aloud
3. To consider the relationship between Medea and Jason
4. To preview the study questions for the Third Episode and Stasimon
5. To familiarize students with the vocabulary for the Third Episode and Stasimon

<u>Activity #1</u>
As a class, briefly review the First Episode and Stasimon and the distinction between "Justified" and "Sympathetic." Remember what Medea said about her position as a woman in Corinthian society.

Next, as a lead-in to the next episode, ask for one or two volunteers from the class to tell a brief story about the aftermath of a breakup. It could be a breakup the student personally experienced or one he or she observed. Remind students that they should keep the identities of the parties anonymous or fictionalized. The important thing is to report the way the two people in the relationship treated each other, and why.

<u>Activity #2</u>
Medea
Jason
Chorus (several students)

Assign the parts listed above to some of the students in your class. Read up to the end of the Second Episode and Stasimon orally.

<u>Activity #3</u>
Now that you have seen Medea's relationship with Creon and her relationship with Jason, it's time for the three of them to get some therapy…on TV.

Choose students to be Medea, Jason, Creon, the host, and the therapist. Set up several chairs and have the host call Medea out to the "stage." Ask Medea how she is feeling. Then, call Creon out so that the therapist can examine Creon and Medea's relationship. Use the following questions to guide the session:

1) Describe the relationship. Is there trust? Mutual respect? Why or why not?
2) Who do you think has more power in the relationship?
3) Where does this person's power come from, in your opinion?
4) What might be done to improve the relationship?
5) Can you think of anything nice to say about the other person?

Next, bring Jason onstage and question him about his relationship with Medea, again using the above questions.

Conclude the show with a recommendation to Creon and Medea about fixing their relationship, then a recommendation for Jason and Medea.

Activity #4
Review the study questions and vocabulary for the Third Episode and Stasimon orally together in class. Tell students that they should read the Third Episode and Stasimon prior to the next class period. Give them the remainder of this class (if time remains) to complete this assignment.

LESSON SIX

Objectives
1. To review the Second Episode and Stasimon
2. To read the Third Episode and Stasimon aloud
3. To consider the function of the Aegeus episode within the play
4. To preview the study questions for the Fourth Episode and Stasimon
5. To familarize students with the vocabulary for the Fourth Episode and Stasimon

Activity #1
As a class, briefly review the Second Episode and Stasimon. Come up with a few words to describe Medea's character based on what you have seen so far. Recall what she has resolved to do. What does she need to accomplish her plan at this point?

Activity #2
Medea
Aegeus
Chorus (several students)

Assign the parts listed above to some of the students in your class. Read the Third Episode up to the exit of Aegeus orally.

Activity #3
Medea tricks Aegeus into helping her by offering him infertility drugs, though she knows that his problem can be easily solved without her. Ask one student to describe an incident of verbal deception he or she has witnessed or experienced. Ask the student how the act made him/her feel about the deceiver. Use the answer to lead into a brief discussion of Medea's character. How does her trickery of Aegeus, who seems like a nice man, make the audience feel about her? Is there any justification for her deception?

Activity #4
Complete reading of the rest of the Third Episode and Stasimon aloud.

Activity #5
Immediately after students finish reading the Third Stasimon, ask the Chorus to describe some of the emotions they are feeling—in single words, if possible. Write these words on the board/overhead/screen. Then, ask Medea to describe some of her emotions, and write these words down as well.

Activity #6
Write the following story elements on the board. As a class, decide which scene/incident makes up each of the following:

Exposition

Conflict

Rising action

Then, draw a line on the board, and mark each scene/incident on the line. Now, decide where the Aegeus episode fits on this line and write it in. What is its function within the play?

Activity #7
Review the study questions and vocabulary for the Fourth Episode and Stasimon orally together in class. Tell students that they should read the Fourth Episode and Stasimon prior to the next class period. Give them the remainder of this class (if time remains) to complete this assignment.

LESSON SEVEN

Objectives
1. To review the Third Episode and Stasimon
2. To read the Fourth Episode and Stasimon aloud
3. To further analyze the relationship between Medea and Jason
4. To preview the study questions for the Fifth Episode and Stasimon
5. To familiarize students with the vocabulary in the Fifth Episode and Stasimon

Activity #1
As a class, briefly review the Third Episode and Stasimon and then the play up to this point. Medea has had conversations with three different men. Trace how she has formulated her plan based on information from each of them.

Activity #2
Medea
Jason
Children (2)
Tutor
Chorus (several students)

Assign the parts listed above to some of the students in your class. Read up to the end of the Fourth Episode and Stasimon orally.

Activity #3
Break the class into small groups. Each group will imagine what the relationship between Medea and Jason was like prior to the beginning of the play. Each group should use evidence from the text to evaluate the relationship and construct a timeline of it. Why might each character have decided to marry the other? When did feelings change on either side?

Each group should present its relationship timeline to the rest of the class, giving an explanation as to how the relationship got to this point.

Activity #4
Review the study questions and vocabulary for the Fifth Episode and Stasimon orally together in class. Tell students that they should read the Fifth Episode and Stasimon prior to the next class period. Give them the remainder of this class (if time remains) to complete this assignment.

LESSON EIGHT

<u>Objectives</u>
1. To review the Fourth Episode and Stasimon
2. To read the Fifth Episode and Stasimon aloud
3. To understand dramatic irony and how it is used
4. To preview the study questions for the Exodus
5. To familiarize students with the vocabulary in the Exodus

<u>Activity #1</u>
As a class, briefly review the Fourth Episode and Stasimon and then the play up to this point. What did the Chorus say? What is Medea's state of mind at this point?

<u>Activity #2</u>
Tutor
Medea
Messenger
Chorus (several students)
Children (2)
Jason

Assign the parts listed above to some of the students in your class. Read up to the end of the Fifth Episode and Stasimon orally.

<u>Activity #3</u>
In *Medea*, there are several instances of dramatic irony. Sometimes the Chorus is present, and both the Chorus and the audience know something that a character (like Jason) does not. When the Tutor comes to tell Medea that the gifts have been accepted, we and Medea know that the news is bad, but the Tutor does not. What the Tutor says even highlights this irony.

Fill out the chart for instances of irony in the play.

<u>Activity #4</u>
Review the study questions and vocabulary for the Exodus orally together in class. Tell students that they should read the Exodus prior to the next class period. Give them the remainder of this class (if time remains) to complete this assignment.

DRAMATIC IRONY CHART

Dramatic Irony occurs when the audience is aware of something that a character does not know. Analyze the dramatic irony in *Medea* by completing the chart. When the Tutor returns with the children, who is "in the know"? Who isn't? What is it that the second character does not know, and how is this emphasized? Write the answers to the questions under "*Medea*." Then, think of another work of literature, a movie, or a television show that has utilized dramatic irony. Write that information under "Other Work." Finally, if you can think of a time in your own life when you (and others) knew something that another person didn't, fill in the information under "Personal."

	Medea	Other Work	Personal
Character Who Knows			
Character Who Doesn't Know			
What is Not Known			
Especially Ironic Statements/Actions			

LESSON NINE

Objectives
1. To review the Fifth Episode and Stasimon
2. To read the Exodus aloud
3. To review film versions of *Medea*
4. To discuss the meaning of Tragic Odes

Activity #1
As a class, briefly review the Fifth Episode and Stasimon and then the play up to this point.

Activity #2
Medea
Jason
Chorus (several students)

Assign the parts listed above to some of the students in your class. Read up to the end of the Exodus orally.

Activity #3
Before this class begins, obtain one or two film versions of *Medea* from the library. When the class is finished reading the Exodus aloud, take a look at the way the scene is done in these versions. Discuss the the director's choices about the final scene.

Activity #4
After watching the film versions, divide students into small groups. Give each group a copy of the "Tragic Odes" questions. Use the rest of the class to discuss the odes and the meaning of tragedy.

TRAGIC ODES

Sophocles was another of the three most famous Greek playwrights. In his play *Oedipus Rex*, the main character, Oedipus, learns that he killed his own father and married his mother. Horrified by this realization, Oedipus blinds himself.

Read the following ode, which is spoken by the Chorus right after Oedipus confronts the truth:

CHORUS:

Oh, the generations of man—
while you live, I count you
as worthless, equal to nothing.
For who, what man
wins more happiness than
just its shape
and the ruin when that shape collapses?
With your example, your fate, your self,
suffering Oedipus,
I call nothing of mortals blessed.

He shot with unsurpassed aim
and gained every kind of
happiness, o Zeus; destroying
the riddle-singer,
the maiden with twisted talons,
like a tower
he stood and defended my land from death.
Since that time he has been called my king
and beyond all men
was honored, ruling in glorious Thebes.

But now, who could be called
more wretched, more bound to toil and wild madness,
more the paradigm of life's reversals?
Oh, famous Oedipus,
you alone sufficed to lie
as son, father, and bridegroom;
how was it, how, poor man,
could your paternal furrows
bear you in such long silence?

All-seeing time discovered you unwilling,
it judged long ago your marriage that is no marriage,
you, both the siring and sired.
Alas, o child of Laius,

if only, if only we had never
set eyes on you!
My grief is like a libation poured from my mouth.
But to speak the truth, because of you I could breath
again
and because of you I sink my eyes into sleep.

Now reread the final words spoken by the Chorus in *Medea*.

Summarize the main idea expressed by each choral ode.

_____

_____

_____

_____

What view does the Chorus have of existence and the gods?

_____

_____

_____

_____

Using ideas from these odes, define *tragedy*.

_____

_____

_____

_____

LESSON TEN

Objectives
1. To evaluate students' understanding of the material
2. To give students the opportunity to practice their personal interaction skills in a small group setting
3. To give students the opportunity to practice their public speaking skills

Activity #1
Divide the class into five groups. Each group should be assigned one of the following topics:

1. Women's roles
2. Foreigners/xenophobia
3. Parenthood
4. Exile
5. Moderation

Each group will review the play and find all the references to its topic. Students should jot down their findings.

When the groups are done with their research, they should discuss their findings. Based on their research, they should try to draw some conclusions about the topic.

Activity #2
Each group will each report its findings and conclusions to the whole class. One student in each group should be appointed to present the group's findings and conclusions.

The teacher or a student should write down on the board or overhead all of the findings and conclusions.

LESSON ELEVEN

Objectives
1. To conclude the theme reports and discussion from Lesson Ten
2. To give students time to review their notes
3. To work on the Greek History reading assignment

Activity #1
Continue any reports and discussion not completed in Lesson Ten. Be sure to continue writing down all important information for students to copy into their notes as study materials.

Activity #2
If you still have time remaining after the discussions, allow students to compare, correct, and revise their notes and/or work on their Greek history assignments. If you are certain that you will have time left over, make arrangements for your class to go to the library to get suitable reading material for the assignment.

LESSON TWELVE

Objectives
1. To distribute Writing Assignment #1
2. To give students an opportunity to incorporate the teacher's suggestions into their papers
3. To evaluate students' individual writing

Activity #1

Distribute Writing Assignment #1. Discuss the directions orally in detail. Allow the remaining class time for students to complete the activity.

If students do not have enough class time to finish, the papers may be collected at the beginning of the next class period.

WRITING ASSIGNMENT #1

PROMPT

Your assignment is to take the information about one of the ideas we've discussed and write an essay about it. Your research has been done through group work, reports, and discussion. Now, take that information and shape it into a well-developed essay.

PREWRITING

One way to start is to decide which of the five topics that have been discussed most interests you. Review your notes, and give the topic some more thought. Jot down ideas relevant to your topic. Then, pick out the three best points. Organize any other thoughts you've put down to see if they can be used as supporting examples or statements for any of your three main points.

DRAFTING

A diagram of a basic, five-paragraph essay might look like this:

1. introduce essay topic
2. main idea (topic sentence) followed by examples or details supporting main idea
3. main idea (topic sentence) followed by examples or details supporting main idea
4. main idea (topic sentence) followed by examples or details supporting main idea
5. summary/closing

Once you have mastered the basic skills of creating a main topic, supporting that topic with main ideas of substance, and explaining those main ideas with examples or details, a whole new world of creativity opens up to you. Then, you can perfect your style of writing, choosing a method of conveying your ideas.

PROMPT

When you finish the rough draft of your essay, ask a classmate to read it. After reading your rough draft, your classmate should tell you what he or she likes best about your work, which parts were difficult to understand, and the way in which your work could be improved. Reread your essay, and, considering your critic's comments, make the corrections you think are necessary.

PROOFREADING

Do a final proofreading of your paper, double-checking your grammar, spelling, organization, and the clarity of your ideas.

WRITING EVALUATION FORM – *MEDEA*

Name: _____ **Date:** _____ **Writing Assignment #** _____

Grade: _____

Circle One For Each Item:

Grammar:	excellent	good	fair	poor
Spelling:	excellent	good	fair	poor
Punctuation:	excellent	good	fair	poor
Legibility:	excellent	good	fair	poor
_____:	excellent	good	fair	poor
_____:	excellent	good	fair	poor

Strengths:

_____
_____
_____

Weaknesses:

_____
_____
_____

Comments/Suggestions:

_____
_____
_____
_____
_____

LESSON THIRTEEN

Objectives
1. To review the main ideas presented in *Medea*
2. To begin the group assignment
3. To give students the opportunity to practice creative writing
4. To give students experience in cooperation and compromise

Activity #1
Explain to students that in the next couple of class periods they will be coming up with their own film version of one scene in *Medea*. Bringing this together will involve three stages of work: preparation (deciding what different elements need to be covered and who should work on them), production (working out how these should be put together), and the actual filming (if possible).

Activity #2
As a class, students will choose the scene they want to develop. Then, divide the class into groups. Assign an element of the film (lighting, music, choreography, costumes/makeup, set design, writing) to each group.

Activity #3
Next, each group will work on its particular area. For lighting: when should the light be brightest, and when should it be low? The costume group should do some research on the costumes that would have been worn by the ancient Greek actors and then decide if this production should be historically accurate or more modern. Similarly, the choreography group might do research how the Chorus would have sang and danced and plan the choreography accordingly.

Groups must write or draw their plans for presentation to the class.

LESSON FOURTEEN

Objectives
1. To complete the group assignment from Lesson Thirteen
2. To analyze the film version(s) of *Medea*
3. To review the production

Activity #1
Each group should briefly explain to the class how it will treat its assigned element in the scene. Then, the whole class will join in a discussion to put all of the elements together. If possible, stage the scene and film it or perform it in class. If that is not possible, watch a film version of the play (or just that scene) to see how the material has been handled.

Activity #2
Distribute a copy of the *Medea* Film Review worksheet to each student. After the class production, have each student use the worksheet to evaluate the production. If you watch another version of the play, use the worksheet to evaluate it as well.

Students should fill out the worksheet by rating each production on a scale of 1-5 (1 being the best, and 5 the worst) and writing down brief notes explaining each rating. When they have finished with their worksheets, ask for some volunteers to share their ratings with the class.

MEDEA FILM REVIEW

Use the worksheet to evaluate the class production of *Medea*. If you watch another version of the play, use the worksheet to evaluate it as well.

Complete the worksheet by rating each production on a scale of 1-5 (1 being the best, and 5 being the worst) and writing down brief notes explaining each rating.

	Production 1	**Production 2**	**Production 3**
Scene:			
Writing			
Acting			
Sound			
Costume			
Choreography			
Lighting			
Other Notes			

LESSON FIFTEEN

Objectives
1. To distribute Writing Assignment #2
2. To have students interpret *Medea* through modern methods of communication
3. To evaluate students' writing
4. To have students revise their Writing Assignment #1 papers

Activity #1
Distribute Writing Assignment #2, and discuss the directions in detail. Give students this class period to work on the assignment, and give them the date the assignment is due.

Activity #2
Call students to your desk (or some other private area) to discuss their papers from Writing Assignment #1. A Writing Evaluation Form is included with this unit to help structure your conferences.

While waiting to be called for a conference, students may work on Writing Assignment #2. After students have had a writing conference with you, they should return to their seats and begin working on their writing assignment revisions while your suggestions are fresh in their minds. Be sure to give students a day and a date when their revisions are due.

WRITING ASSIGNMENT #2

PROMPT

Communication occurs on several levels in *Medea*. To understand the play, it is important to know what the characters seem to be saying and what they are actually saying.

In this assignment, you will pretend to be one of the main characters in *Medea*. You will choose one of the dialogues in which your character speaks and reinterpret it using modern methods of communication. For example, you might choose to be Medea trying to persuade Creon not to send you into exile. Will you email or text Creon? Will you post something on a social-networking site?

Choose from one of the following dialogues:

1. conversation between Medea and Jason (first or second)

2. conversation between the Tutor and Nurse or the Nurse and Chorus

3. conversation between Creon and Medea

4. conversation between Messenger and Medea

5. conversation between Aegeus and Medea

Write the conversation as it might appear if these characters were around today—through email, Facebook, Twitter, texting, instant messaging, or whatever means of communication you use with friends and family. You can use as many of these forms as you like; the point is to imagine yourself, in the present day, communicating with other characters in *Medea*.

PREWRITING & PLANNING

One way to start is to summarize the conversation in your own words. Jot down notes about how each character feels about the different points made in the conversation.

Then, think about the different ways you communicate with family and friends. Do you choose to use certain methods when delivering different kinds of information (i.e., bad or very serious news, for instance)? Which methods would you choose if you were the characters in this scene from *Medea*?

In addition, are there times when you say one thing, but mean something else? How can the person with whom you are communicating know this?

WRITING

Write out the conversation using the method(s) you have chosen. If you choose something like Facebook or Twitter, try to include the responses of other characters. Be as creative as you like.

PROMPT

When you have finished a draft of your interpretation, ask a classmate to review it. After reading the draft, your classmate should tell you what he or she likes best about your work, which parts seem unrealistic or confusing, and what improvements could be made overall. Reread your paper, and, taking into consideration your classmate's comments, make the corrections you think are necessary.

PROOFREADING

Do a final proofreading of your interpretation to double-check that it says what you want it to say.

WRITING EVALUATION FORM – *MEDEA*

Name: _____ **Date:** _____ **Writing Assignment #** ____

Grade: _____

Circle One For Each Item:

Grammar:	excellent	good	fair	poor
Spelling:	excellent	good	fair	poor
Punctuation:	excellent	good	fair	poor
Legibility:	excellent	good	fair	poor
_____:	excellent	good	fair	poor
_____:	excellent	good	fair	poor

Strengths:

_____

_____

_____

Weaknesses:

_____

_____

_____

Comments/Suggestions:

_____

_____

_____

_____

_____

LESSON SIXTEEN

Objectives
1. To cover important ideas presented in *Medea*
2. To focus on interpretive, critical, and personal responses
3. To enhance students' understanding of *Medea*

Activity #1
Choose the questions from the Extra Discussion Questions/Writing Assignments which seem most appropriate for your students. A class discussion of these questions is most effective if students have been given the opportunity to formulate answers to the questions prior to the discussion. To this end, you may either have all the students formulate answers to all the questions, divide your class into groups and assign one or more questions to each group, or you could assign one question to each student in your class. The option you choose will make a difference in the amount of class time needed for this activity.

Note: The use of graphic organizers may be helpful to students in preparing their answers. Encourage them to use any diagrams or graphics that they feel are necessary.

EXTRA DISCUSSION QUESTIONS *Medea*

Critical

1. Euripides' audience would have known the basic elements of the Medea story. Why, then, does the playwright include the exposition in the Prologue?
2. Explain the function of the chorus in *Medea*. Be sure to consider how Euripides uses the chorus to underscore the themes of the play.
3. What persuasive techniques does Medea use in the play? Consider at least two instances of persuasion, and explain how they might contribute to the plot, characterization, and themes of the play.
4. Analyze Euripides' use of the *deus ex machina* in *Medea*. Why might he have chosen this device, and how successful is it?
5. Explain the function of irony in *Medea*.

Critical/Personal Response

6. Defend either Jason's position or Medea's position. Be sure to refer to the points they each make in their arguments.
7. Compare and contrast the characteristics of Creon and Aegeus.
8. What is the climax of the play? Be sure to support your answer.

Personal Response

9. Do you consider Medea a tragic hero? Defend your opinion. Include your definition of a hero.
10. Explore some different views of parenthood in *Medea*. Which one do you most agree with, and why?

LESSON SEVENTEEN

<u>Objectives</u>
1. To expand students' knowledge of the topics addressed in this unit
2. To review students' Greek History reading assignments

<u>Activity #1</u>
Ask each student to give a brief oral report about the topic he or she researched for the Greek history assignment. You may have students present a complete report without using notes, or you may have students read directly from written report, or something in between these two options.

Start with one student's report. Then, ask if anyone else in the class has read about a topic related to the first student's report. If no one has, choose another student at random. After each report, be sure to ask if anyone has a report related to the one just completed. This will help keep a continuity during the discussion of the reports.

LESSON EIGHTEEN

<u>Objectives</u>
To review all of the vocabulary work done in this unit

<u>Activity #1</u>
Choose one (or more) of the vocabulary review activities listed below and spend your class period as directed in the activity. Some of the materials for these review activities are located in the Vocabulary Resource Materials section in this LitPlan.

VOCABULARY REVIEW ACTIVITIES

1. Divide your class into two teams and have an old-fashioned spelling or definition bee.

2. Give each of your students (or students in groups of two, three, or four) a *Medea* Vocabulary Word Search Puzzle. The person (group) to find all of the vocabulary words in the puzzle first wins.

3. Give students a *Medea* Vocabulary Word Search Puzzle without the word list. The person or group to find the most vocabulary words in the puzzle wins.

4. Use a *Medea* Vocabulary Crossword Puzzle. Put the puzzle onto a transparency on the overhead projector (so everyone can see it), and do the puzzle together as a class.

5. Give students a *Medea* Vocabulary Matching Worksheet to do.

6. Divide your class into two teams. Use *Medea* vocabulary words with their letters jumbled as a word list. Student 1 from Team A faces off against Student 1 from Team B. You write the first jumbled word on the board. The first student (1A or 1B) to unscramble the word wins the chance for his or her team to score points. If 1A wins the jumble, go to student 2A and give him or her a definition. He or she must give you the correct spelling of the vocabulary word which fits that definition. If he or she does, Team A scores a point, and you give student 3A a definition for which you expect a correctly spelled matching vocabulary word. Continue giving Team A definitions until some team member makes an incorrect response. An incorrect response sends the game back to the jumbled-word face off, this time with students 2A and 2B. Instead of repeating giving definitions to the first few students of each team, continue with the student after the one who gave the last incorrect response on the team. For example, if Team B wins the jumbled-word face-off, and student 5B gave the last incorrect answer for Team B, you would start this round of definition questions with student 6B, and so on. The team with the most points wins!

7. Have students write a story in which they correctly use as many vocabulary words as possible. Have students read their compositions orally. Post the most original compositions on your bulletin board.

LESSON NINETEEN

Objectives
To review the main ideas and events in *Medea*

Activity #1
Choose one of the review games/activities suggested in this unit and spend your class time as directed there.

REVIEW GAMES/ACTIVITIES

1. Ask the class to make up a unit test for *Medea*. The test should have 4 sections: matching, true/false, short answer, and essay. Students may use 1/2 period to make the test and then swap papers and use the other 1/2 class period to take a test a classmate has devised (open book). You may want to use the unit test included in this packet or take questions from the students' unit tests to formulate your own test.

2. Take half a period for students to make up true and false questions (including the answers). Collect the papers and divide the class into two teams. Draw a big tic-tac-toe board on the chalk board. Make one team X and one team O. Ask questions to each side, giving each student one turn. If the question is answered correctly, that students' team's letter (X or O) is placed in the box. If the answer is incorrect, no letter is placed in the box. The object is to get three in a row like tic-tac-toe. You may want to keep track of the number of games won for each team.

3. Take half a period for students to make up questions (true/false and short answer). Collect the questions. Divide the class into two teams. You'll alternate asking questions to individual members of teams A & B (like in a spelling bee). The question keeps going from A to B until it is correctly answered, then a new question is asked. A correct answer does not allow the team to get another question. Correct answers are +2 points; incorrect answers are -1 point.

4. Have students pair up and quiz each other from their study guides and class notes.

5. Give students a *Medea* crossword puzzle to complete.

6. Play "What's My Line?". This is similar to the old television show. Students assume the roles of different characters from the story. One student gives clues to the class, or to a panel of contestants. The contestants try to guess the identity of the guest. Students may enjoy assisting you in creating rules and procedures for the game.

7. Divide your class into two teams. Use *Medea* crossword words with their letters jumbled as a word list. Student 1 from Team A faces off against Student 1 from Team B. You write the first jumbled word on the board. The first student (1A or 1B) to unscramble the word wins the chance for his or her team to score points. If 1A wins the jumble, go to student 2A and give him or her a clue. He or she must give you the correct word which matches that clue. If he or she does, Team A scores a point, and you give student 3A a clue for which you expect another correct response. Continue giving Team A clues until some team member makes an incorrect response. An incorrect response sends the game back to the jumbled-word face off, this time with students 2A and 2B. Instead of repeating giving clues to the first few students of each team, continue with the student after the one who gave the last incorrect response on the team. For example, if Team B wins the jumbled-word face-off, and student 5B gave the last incorrect answer for Team B, you would start this round of clue questions with student 6B, and so on. The team with the most points wins!

8. Play Jeopardy. Divide the class into two groups. Assign each group a category from the story and have them devise answers for that category. Play the game according to the television show procedures.

9. Play Drawing in the Details. This is similar to "Pictionary." Divide students into teams. A student from one team draws a scene from the story. (You may want to specify the section.) Drawings should be kept simple, to keep the pace lively. Students in the opposing team locate the scene in their books and read it aloud. If they are incorrect, the illustrator's team has a chance to guess. Involve students in setting up a scoring system and any other necessary rules.

Activity #2
Remind students that the Unit Test will be given in the next class meeting. Assign the review of the Study Guides and students' class notes for homework.

LESSON TWENTY

Objectives
1. To test the students' understanding of the main ideas and themes in *Medea*
2. To improve students' writing skills
3. To distribute Writing Assignment #3

Activity #1
Distribute the unit tests. Go over the instructions in detail and allow students the entire class period to complete the exam.

NOTES ABOUT THE UNIT TESTS IN THIS UNIT:

There are 5 different unit tests included in the LitPlan Teacher Pack. Two are short answer, two are multiple choice. There is one advanced short answer test. The answers to the advanced short answer test will be based on the discussions you have had during class and should be graded accordingly. You should choose the tests and/or test parts which best suit your needs. Matching and short answer tests have answer keys. For essay type questions, grade according to your own criteria based on class discussions and the level of your students. Also, you will need to choose vocabulary words to read orally for the vocabulary section of the short answer tests.

Activity #2
While students are working on the unit tests, distribute Writing Assignment #3. After students complete their tests, they should begin working on this assignment.

Note: You may omit the "Composition" section of the test and use this writing assignment instead, if you prefer.

Activity #3
Collect all test papers and assigned books prior to the end of the class period.

WRITING ASSIGNMENT #3

PROMPT

You have read *Medea*, had discussions about the ideas and characters presented in the play, and have become educated about a variety of topics related to it. Now, thinking about all you have learned, make an argument as to which major character in *Medea* is the most sympathetic. Be specific, and use examples from the text to support your ideas.

PREWRITING

One way to start is to list all the major characters. Next to the name of each character, jot down all the reasons he or she might seem sympathetic to the audience. Then, looking at that information, decide which character is most sympathetic.

DRAFTING

Your introductory paragraph could contain information about those who are partly justified in their actions, followed by something like, "but the most sympathetic character in *Medea* is _____."

Following the introductory paragraph, the paragraphs in the body of your paper should each give a reason why you think that character is sympathetic. Within each paragraph, you should support your statements with as many facts and examples from the text as possible.

Your last paragraph should give your final thoughts and conclusions.

PROMPT

When you finish the rough draft of your paper, ask a classmate to read it. After reading your rough draft, your classmate should tell you what he or she likes best about your work, which parts are difficult to understand, and in what ways your work could be improved. Reread your paper, and, considering your critic's comments, make the corrections you think are necessary.

PROOFREADING

Do a final proofreading of your paper, double-checking your grammar, spelling, organization, and the clarity of your ideas.

WRITING EVALUATION FORM – *MEDEA*

Name: _____ **Date:** _____ **Writing Assignment #** ____

Grade: _____

Circle One For Each Item:

Grammar:	excellent	good	fair	poor
Spelling:	excellent	good	fair	poor
Punctuation:	excellent	good	fair	poor
Legibility:	excellent	good	fair	poor
_____:	excellent	good	fair	poor
_____:	excellent	good	fair	poor

Strengths:

_____
_____
_____

Weaknesses:

_____
_____
_____

Comments/Suggestions:

_____
_____
_____
_____
_____

UNIT TESTS

Medea Short-Answer Unit Test 1

I. Matching

____ 1. MEDEA   A. spoken lines; takes place between odes

____ 2. ARGO   B. the holy place where Aegeus goes to receive advice from the gods

____ 3. TUTOR   C. the part of the play before the Chorus enters

____ 4. CHORUS   D. Jason's second wife; she dies from a poisoned dress.

____ 5. PRINCESS   E. Jason's ship

____ 6. NURSE   F. tells the Nurse about Medea's exile

____ 7. JASON   G. a group of characters that acts as one

____ 8. ORACLE   H. Greek term for ode; takes place between dramatic episodes

____ 9. PROLOGUE   I. Medea's servant; wants a life of moderation

____ 10. EPISODE   J. murders her children, the princess, and Creon

____ 11. STASIMON   K. Medea's unfaithful husband

II. Short Answer

1. Where did Medea come from originally?

2. What happened to Pelias, and who was responsible for it?

3. What bad news does the Tutor bring to the Nurse?

4. What clue do we get from Medea herself about her capacity to commit violent acts?

5. According to Medea, what problems do women face?

6. What promise does Medea extract from the Chorus?

7. What does Medea say about cleverness?

8. Why does Creon allow Medea to stay in the country for one day?

9. According to Jason, why has he come to see Medea before she leaves?

10. Explain Jason's rationale for his poor treatment of Medea.

11. What plan does Medea come up with to kill the princess?

12. Who takes the gifts to the princess?

13. What is the first thing the Messenger urges Medea to do?

14. Where is Medea when Jason last sees her?

15. What kind of love is best, according to the Chorus?

16. How will Athens treat Medea, according to the Chorus?

III. Quotations: Explain the importance and meaning of the following quotations:

1. Alas!
   I have suffered, oh, dreadfully
   have I suffered things
   worthy of lamentation.

2. ...I declare that you must leave
   this land in exile, taking your two children
   with you, and don't delay at all.

3. O fatherland, O home, never let me be
   without my city,
   leading a life of impossibility, difficult
   to endure, the most pitiful of pains.

4. This is how it is with me: When you come
   to my land, I will try to help you with
   justice on my side.

5. Allow me to bury and mourn these corpses.

IV. Composition
1. In a well-developed essay, consider Medea as an outsider. What puts her in this position, and how does it affect her? Why might Euripides emphasize these qualities?

2. Explore some different views of parenthood in *Medea*. Which one do you most agree with, and why?

V. Vocabulary
   Write the vocabulary words you are given. After writing them down, go back and write in their definitions.

Word	Definition
1	
2	
3	
4	
5	
6	
7	
8	
9	
10	

Medea Short-Answer Unit Test 1 Answer Key

I. Matching

J	1.	MEDEA	A.	spoken lines; takes place between odes
E	2.	ARGO	B.	the holy place where Aegeus goes to receive advice from the gods
F	3.	TUTOR	C.	the part of the play before the Chorus enters
G	4.	CHORUS	D.	Jason's second wife; she dies from a poisoned dress.
D	5.	PRINCESS	E.	Jason's ship
I	6.	NURSE	F.	tells the Nurse about Medea's exile
K	7.	JASON	G.	a group of characters that acts as one
B	8.	ORACLE	H.	Greek term for ode; takes place between dramatic episodes
C	9.	PROLOGUE	I.	Medea's servant; wants a life of moderation
A	10.	EPISODE	J.	murders her children, the princess, and Creon
H	11.	STASIMON	K.	Medea's unfaithful husband

II. Short Answer

1. Where did Medea come from originally?
   Colchis

2. What happened to Pelias, and who was responsible for it?
   Medea tricked Pelias' daughters into killing him.

3. What bad news does the Tutor bring to the Nurse?
   He has heard a rumor that Medea and her children will be exiled from Corinth.

4. What clue do we get from Medea herself about her capacity to commit violent acts?
   Medea killed her own brother to get away from her father, so she seems to be capable of anything.

5. According to Medea, what problems do women face?
   Women have to buy marriage with dowries. Once they are married, they give up all power to their husbands. Society forces women to stay within their marriages whether or not they are happy. Women have no way of knowing whether they will be happy before they get married, and no one teaches them how to deal with men. Furthermore, marriage can endanger their lives; they may die in childbirth, or their husbands may be violent.

6. What promise does Medea extract from the Chorus?
   The Chorus will keep silent about Medea's plans for revenge against Jason.

7. What does Medea say about cleverness?
   Cleverness never benefits anyone—a clever person is useless among stupid people, and suspect among others.

8. Why does Creon allow Medea to stay in the country for one day?
   He reasons that one day is not long enough for her to do anything terrible.

9. According to Jason, why has he come to see Medea before she leaves?
   Jason says that he is trying to make sure that Medea and the children are provided for.

10. Explain Jason's rationale for his poor treatment of Medea.
    Jason says that marrying the princess will benefit everyone; he can join the two families so that they will all be well off.

11. What plan does Medea come up with to kill the princess?
    She will tell Jason she has made peace with his new marriage and then have her sons deliver to the princess a dress and crown laced with poison. The princess will die when she wears these items.

12. Who takes the gifts to the princess?
    Medea sends the children to give her the gifts.

13. What is the first thing the Messenger urges Medea to do?
    He tells Medea to run away immediately.

14. Where is Medea when Jason last sees her?
    She is flying over Jason's head in a chariot pulled by dragons.

15. What kind of love is best, according to the Chorus?
    The Chorus praises love in moderation. Excessive love, like Medea's, is dangerous.

16. How will Athens treat Medea, according to the Chorus?
    The Chorus cannot fathom how a place as holy as Athens can take in someone who has done something as unholy as killing her own children.

Medea Short-Answer Unit Test 2

I. Matching

____ 1. CORINTH   A. king of the Gods; Medea prays to him.

____ 2. COLCHIS   B. pull Medea's chariot

____ 3. PELIAS   C. King of Troezen; Aegeus wants to consult him.

____ 4. CREON   D. the first entrance of the Chorus

____ 5. CHILDREN   E. didn't give women music—they might sing about the badness of men.

____ 6. AEGEUS   F. Medea's hometown

____ 7. ZEUS   G. murdered by his own daughters

____ 8. DRAGONS   H. the town where Medea lives

____ 9. PHOEBUS   I. king of Corinth; father of the princess

____ 10. PITTHEUS   J. king of Athens; promises Medea safe harbor

____ 11. PARODOS   K. take gifts to the princess; murdered by Medea

II. Short Answer

1. Where does the play take place?

2. According to the Nurse, why is Medea miserable?

3. What does the Nurse say about powerful people?

4. To whom does Medea pray? Why is this significant?

5. What does Medea blame for her unhappiness?

6. Describe Creon's manner of speaking. Is he direct or indirect?

7. What does Medea promise Creon?

8. What potential problem does Medea see in murdering her enemies directly?

9. What are some of the things Medea has done for Jason?

10. What problem did Aegeus ask the oracle about, and what response did he get?

11. How does the Chorus respond to Medea's plan?

12. Why does Jason initially refuse the gifts? How does Medea convince him to accept them?

13. How does Creon die?

14. What does Jason beg of Medea? What is her reply?

15. What topic does the second part of the stasimon address?

16. According to the Chorus, why is the delivery of the gifts the point of no return?

III. Quotations: Explain the importance and meaning of the following quotations:

1. This is the greatest salvation,
   when a wife stands together with her husband.
   But, now it's all hate, what was dearest is sick,
   for Jason betrayed his children and my mistress
   and goes to bed with a royal marriage.

2. Of all things that live and have intelligence,
   we women are the most wretched creatures.

3. I saved you, as all the Greeks know who sailed
   with you on your ship, the Argo.

4. ...I call the gods to witness how I
   would do anything to help you and the children,
   but good things don't please you.

5. Since you shared your plan with us, I want to
   help you and aid the laws of humanity:
   please don't do this.

IV. Composition
1. In a well-developed essay, consider Medea as an outsider. What puts her in this position, and how does it affect her? Why might Euripides emphasize these qualities?

2. Defend either Jason's position or Medea's position. Be sure to refer to the points they each make in their arguments.

V. Vocabulary
   Write the vocabulary words you are given. After writing them down, go back and write in their definitions.

Word	Definition
1	
2	
3	
4	
5	
6	
7	
8	
9	
10	

Medea Short-Answer Unit Test 2 Answer Key

I. Matching

H	1.	CORINTH	A.	king of the Gods; Medea prays to him.
F	2.	COLCHIS	B.	pull Medea's chariot
G	3.	PELIAS	C.	King of Troezen; Aegeus wants to consult him.
I	4.	CREON	D.	the first entrance of the Chorus
K	5.	CHILDREN	E.	didn't give women music—they might sing about the badness of men.
J	6.	AEGEUS	F.	Medea's hometown
A	7.	ZEUS	G.	murdered by his own daughters
B	8.	DRAGONS	H.	the town where Medea lives
E	9.	PHOEBUS	I.	king of Corinth; father of the princess
C	10.	PITTHEUS	J.	king of Athens; promises Medea safe harbor
D	11.	PARODOS	K.	take gifts to the princess; murdered by Medea

II. Short Answer

1. Where does the play take place?
   Corinth

2. According to the Nurse, why is Medea miserable?
   Jason, Medea's husband, has abandoned her to marry the daughter of Creon, the king of Corinth.

3. What does the Nurse say about powerful people?
   The Nurse says that power is bad for human beings; when powerful people get angry, they do a lot of damage. She prefers a life of moderation.

4. To whom does Medea pray? Why is this significant?
   Medea prays to Zeus and Themis. Zeus is king of the gods, and Themis is the goddess of oaths. These are not trivial prayers—Medea is calling upon two powerful deities.

5. What does Medea blame for her unhappiness?
   Medea says that her behavior is not proper for a foreigner or native citizen, but she can't help herself; the situation is too upsetting.

6. Describe Creon's manner of speaking. Is he direct or indirect?
   Creon is direct; he gets right to the point. He tells Medea that she has to leave immediately.

7. What does Medea promise Creon?
   Medea promises she will not injure him.

8. What potential problem does Medea see in murdering her enemies directly?
   She might get caught in the act and stopped. Everyone would laugh at her.

9. What are some of the things Medea has done for Jason?
   Medea helped Jason kill the dragon that was guarding the Golden Fleece, she betrayed her father in order to marry Jason, and she had Pelias brutally murdered.

10. What problem did Aegeus ask the oracle about, and what response did he get?
    Aegeus wants to have a child. The oracle told him not to "loosen the wineskin's protruding foot" before he got home (i.e., not to have intercourse before getting home).

11. How does the Chorus respond to Medea's plan?
    The Chorus is horrified and begs Medea to reconsider her decision.

12. Why does Jason initially refuse the gifts? How does Medea convince him to accept them?
    Jason says that the princess does not need any more dresses. Medea tells him that the dresses may play a part in getting the children's exile repealed.

13. How does Creon die?
    When Creon embraces his dead daughter, the dress clings to him, and the poison rubs off on him.

14. What does Jason beg of Medea? What is her reply?
    He begs to be allowed to bury his children. Medea refuses; she tells him she will bury them herself.

15. What topic does the second part of the stasimon address?
    The Chorus discusses exile from one's native land, calling it the most terrible thing a person can go through.

16. According to the Chorus, why is the delivery of the gifts the point of no return?
    Knowing Medea's character and intention, the Chorus is aware that the delivery of gifts to the princess seals the fate of the children.

Medea Advanced Short-Answer Unit Test

I. Matching

____ 1. MEDEA   A. take gifts to the princess; murdered by Medea

____ 2. COLCHIS   B. Jason's second wife; she dies from a poisoned dress.

____ 3. PELIAS   C. tells the Nurse about Medea's exile

____ 4. TUTOR   D. Medea's hometown

____ 5. CHILDREN   E. murdered by his own daughters

____ 6. ZEUS   F. king of the Gods; Medea prays to him.

____ 7. PRINCESS   G. murders her children, the princess, and Creon

II. Short Answer
1. Euripides' audience would have known the basic elements of the Medea story. Why, then, does the playwright include the exposition in the Prologue?

2. Explain the function of the Chorus in *Medea*. Be sure to consider how Euripides uses the Chorus to underscore the themes of the play.

3. Analyze the different views we get of Medea in the Prologue and Parodos. How are they alike, and how are they different? Why does Euripides provide multiple perspectives?

4. In a well-developed essay, defend either Creon's or Medea's point of view. Make sure you refer to the points each makes in his or her argument.

5. What is the climax of the play? Be sure to support your answer.

6. Analyze Euripides' use of the *deus ex machina* in *Medea*. Why might he have chosen this device, and how successful is it?

7. Compare and contrast the characteristics of Creon and Aegeus.

III. Quotations: Explain the importance and meaning of the following quotations:

1. Do you think I would flatter that man
   if I had no plan or profit in it?

2. Let no one think me
   weak or helpless or calm, but the other sort,
   hard on enemies and kind to friends.

3. I seek pardon and agree that
   I spoke badly then, but I've rethought it all now.

4. And you, wretched man, disastrously
   married to royal kin,
   unknowingly, you are bringing
   mortal destruction to your sons and
   hateful death to your wife.
   Poor man, how much you misunderstand your destiny.

5. I myself with happiness
   followed the boys to the women's quarters.

6. Pollution from relatives is difficult for mortals,
   and it brings grief to kinslayers in tune with
   their crime, falling on their house by god's will.

7. Yes, by the gods, stop it! The time is critical!

8. My grandfather
   the Sun is giving me this chariot,
   for protection against hostile hands.

IV. Composition
1. Explain the function of irony in *Medea*.

2. Explore some different views of parenthood in *Medea*. Which one do you most agree with, and why?

V. Vocabulary
   A. Write the vocabulary words you are given. After writing them down, go back and write in their definitions.

Word	Definition
1	
2	
3	
4	
5	
6	
7	
8	
9	
10	

   B. Write a paragraph about the book using 8 of the 10 vocabulary words above.

Medea Advanced Short-Answer Unit Test Answer Key

I. Matching

G	1.	MEDEA	A.	take gifts to the princess; murdered by Medea
D	2.	COLCHIS	B.	Jason's second wife; she dies from a poisoned dress.
E	3.	PELIAS	C.	tells the Nurse about Medea's exile
C	4.	TUTOR	D.	Medea's hometown
A	5.	CHILDREN	E.	murdered by his own daughters
F	6.	ZEUS	F.	king of the Gods; Medea prays to him.
B	7.	PRINCESS	G.	murders her children, the princess, and Creon

Medea Multiple Choice Unit Test 1

I. Matching

____ 1. MEDEA   A. murders her children, the princess, and Creon
____ 2. COLCHIS   B. a group of characters that acts as one
____ 3. TUTOR   C. take gifts to the princess; murdered by Medea
____ 4. CHORUS   D. Jason's second wife; she dies from a poisoned dress.
____ 5. CHILDREN   E. Medea's hometown
____ 6. ZEUS   F. king of the Gods; Medea prays to him.
____ 7. PRINCESS   G. tells the Nurse about Medea's exile

II. Multiple Choice

1. Where did Medea come from originally?
    A. Sparta
    B. Corinth
    C. Colchis
    D. Athens

2. Where does the play take place?
    A. Athens
    B. Pelias
    C. Colchis
    D. Corinth

3. According to the Nurse, why is Medea miserable?
    A. Medea and Jason have been forbidden to see each other.
    B. Medea is sorry about what happened to Pelias.
    C. Jason abandoned her to marry the daughter of the king of Corinth.
    D. Creon, Jason's uncle, has demanded that Medea marry him.

4. What kind of life does the Nurse want to lead?
    A. a brief, exciting life
    B. a legendary but tragic life
    C. a holy, quiet life
    D. a simple, moderate life

5. What promise does Medea extract from the Chorus?
    A. The Chorus will take care of Medea's children.
    B. The Chorus will get even with Jason for abandoning Medea.
    C. The Chorus will help Medea get out of Corinth.
    D. The Chorus will keep silent about Medea's plans for revenge against Jason.

6. Why does Creon allow Medea to stay in the country for one day?
    A. He needs her to make a potion for him.
    B. He reasons that Medea cannot do anything terrible in one day.
    C. He wants to get back at his daughter for marrying Jason.
    D. He will be leaving Corinth in one day.

7. How has Medea benefited from being married to Jason, according to him?
   A. She has been given citizenship and the right to vote.
   B. She has a room in the palace, and she is best friends with the princess.
   C. She has lived in a civilized place and learned how to use laws.
   D. She has been able to share her culture with the people of Corinth.

8. What problem did Aegeus ask the oracle about?
   A. He is depressed.
   B. He cannot have children.
   C. He wants a divorce.
   D. He cannot sleep.

9. What will Medea use to kill the princess?
   A. a bewitched cup of wine
   B. a poisoned dress
   C. a knife
   D. a noose

10. What is the first thing the Messenger urges Medea to do?
    A. hide in the palace
    B. apologize to the princess
    C. save the children
    D. run away immediately

11. How does Creon die?
    A. The gods strike him down in vengeance for his actions toward Medea.
    B. Upon seeing his dead daughter, he jumps into the sea and drowns.
    C. He gets into a fight with Jason and is fatally stabbed.
    D. When he embraces his dead daughter, the dress clings to him, and the poison kills him.

12. What does Jason beg Medea to do?
    A. apologize to the people of Corinth
    B. allow him to bury his children
    C. stay married to him
    D. kill him also

III. Quotations: Explain the importance and meaning of the following quotations:

1. Alas!
   I have suffered, oh, dreadfully
   have I suffered things
   worthy of lamentation.

2. Do you think I would flatter that man
   if I had no plan or profit in it?

3. I shall send them bearing gifts to her,
   a delicate dress and golden crown.

4. Cheer up! You'll return soon, through your sons' influence.

5. Should I go into the house? I think I should stop the murder for the children.

IV. Vocabulary

____ 1. EXILE   A. anger
____ 2. ABSTRUSE   B. without, lacking
____ 3. RASH   C. low; evil
____ 4. BASE   D. a bridal price
____ 5. BEREFT   E. careless; foolish
____ 6. ENTREAT   F. hard to understand
____ 7. PEERLESS   G. unmatched
____ 8. DOWRY   H. to ask
____ 9. WRATH   I. an outcast
____ 10. EXPIATION   J. repayment for a wrong

V. Composition

1. Explain the function of the Chorus in *Medea*. Be sure to consider how Euripides uses the Chorus to underscore the themes of the play.

2. In a well-developed essay, defend either Creon's or Medea's point of view. Make sure you refer to the points each makes in his or her argument.

Medea Multiple Choice Unit Test 1 Answer Key

I. Matching

A	1. MEDEA	A.	murders her children, the princess, and Creon
E	2. COLCHIS	B.	a group of characters that acts as one
G	3. TUTOR	C.	take gifts to the princess; murdered by Medea
B	4. CHORUS	D.	Jason's second wife; she dies from a poisoned dress.
C	5. CHILDREN	E.	Medea's hometown
F	6. ZEUS	F.	king of the Gods; Medea prays to him.
D	7. PRINCESS	G.	tells the Nurse about Medea's exile

II. Multiple Choice

C 1. Where did Medea come from originally?
   A. Sparta
   B. Corinth
   C. Colchis
   D. Athens

D 2. Where does the play take place?
   A. Athens
   B. Pelias
   C. Colchis
   D. Corinth

C 3. According to the Nurse, why is Medea miserable?
   A. Medea and Jason have been forbidden to see each other.
   B. Medea is sorry about what happened to Pelias.
   C. Jason abandoned her to marry the daughter of the king of Corinth.
   D. Creon, Jason's uncle, has demanded that Medea marry him.

D 4. What kind of life does the Nurse want to lead?
   A. a brief, exciting life
   B. a legendary but tragic life
   C. a holy, quiet life
   D. a simple, moderate life

D 5. What promise does Medea extract from the Chorus?
   A. The Chorus will take care of Medea's children.
   B. The Chorus will get even with Jason for abandoning Medea.
   C. The Chorus will help Medea get out of Corinth.
   D. The Chorus will keep silent about Medea's plans for revenge against Jason.

B 6. Why does Creon allow Medea to stay in the country for one day?
   A. He needs her to make a potion for him.
   B. He reasons that Medea cannot do anything terrible in one day.
   C. He wants to get back at his daughter for marrying Jason.
   D. He will be leaving Corinth in one day.

C 7. How has Medea benefited from being married to Jason, according to him?
   A. She has been given citizenship and the right to vote.
   B. She has a room in the palace, and she is best friends with the princess.
   C. She has lived in a civilized place and learned how to use laws.
   D. She has been able to share her culture with the people of Corinth.

B 8. What problem did Aegeus ask the oracle about?
   A. He is depressed.
   B. He cannot have children.
   C. He wants a divorce.
   D. He cannot sleep.

B 9. What will Medea use to kill the princess?
   A. a bewitched cup of wine
   B. a poisoned dress
   C. a knife
   D. a noose

D 10. What is the first thing the Messenger urges Medea to do?
   A. hide in the palace
   B. apologize to the princess
   C. save the children
   D. run away immediately

D 11. How does Creon die?
   A. The gods strike him down in vengeance for his actions toward Medea.
   B. Upon seeing his dead daughter, he jumps into the sea and drowns.
   C. He gets into a fight with Jason and is fatally stabbed.
   D. When he embraces his dead daughter, the dress clings to him, and the poison kills him.

B 12. What does Jason beg Medea to do?
   A. apologize to the people of Corinth
   B. allow him to bury his children
   C. stay married to him
   D. kill him also

IV. Vocabulary

I	1.	EXILE	A.	anger
F	2.	ABSTRUSE	B.	without, lacking
E	3.	RASH	C.	low; evil
C	4.	BASE	D.	a bridal price
B	5.	BEREFT	E.	careless; foolish
H	6.	ENTREAT	F.	hard to understand
G	7.	PEERLESS	G.	unmatched
D	8.	DOWRY	H.	to ask
A	9.	WRATH	I.	an outcast
J	10.	EXPIATION	J.	repayment for a wrong

Medea Multiple Choice Unit Test 2

I. Matching

____ 1. MEDEA   A. murders her children, the princess, and Creon

____ 2. COLCHIS   B. king of the Gods; Medea prays to him.

____ 3. ARGO   C. pull Medea's chariot

____ 4. CHILDREN   D. take gifts to the princess; murdered by Medea

____ 5. ZEUS   E. Jason's ship

____ 6. PRINCESS   F. Medea's hometown

____ 7. DRAGONS   G. Jason's second wife; she dies from a poisoned dress.

II. Multiple Choice

1. What was the name of Jason's ship?
   A. the *Argo*
   B. the *Mighty Jason*
   C. the *Golden Fleece*
   D. the *Bounty*

2. What happened to Pelias, and who was responsible for it?
   A. Medea poisoned him.
   B. Jason killed him in battle.
   C. Medea tricked Pelias' daughters into killing him.
   D. He died of natural causes; no one was responsible.

3. What bad news does the Tutor bring to the nurse?
   A. Creon has decided that the children no longer need a nurse.
   B. Medea and her children have been exiled from Corinth.
   C. Jason has decided to marry Creon's daughter.
   D. Medea is unhappy in Corinth and wants to go home.

4. What does the Nurse say about power?
   A. Power is good for men, but not for women.
   B. Power is dangerous and can cause harm.
   C. People like power and should have it.
   D. People abuse power, but should still have it.

5. Why does Creon exile Medea?
   A. He has been told to do so by the oracle.
   B. He fears that she will harm him or his family.
   C. He thinks she is someone else.
   D. He does not like Jason.

6. What does Medea do to try to persuade Creon to let her stay?
   A. She embraces Creon's knees.
   B. She prays to Zeus.
   C. She gives him a gold crown.
   D. She offers him her children.

7. Why does Creon allow Medea to stay in the country for one day?
    A. He will be leaving Corinth in one day.
    B. He needs her to make a potion for him.
    C. He reasons that Medea cannot do anything terrible in one day.
    D. He wants to get back at his daughter for marrying Jason.

8. Which of the following is NOT something Medea did for Jason, according to the speech she makes?
    A. She betrayed her father in order to marry Jason.
    B. She allowed Jason to divorce her and marry Creon's daughter.
    C. She helped Jason kill the dragon that was guarding the Golden Fleece.
    D. She had Pelias brutally murdered.

9. What does Medea make Aegeus promise to do?
    A. adopt her children
    B. talk to Creon for her
    C. give her safe harbor
    D. leave her all his money

10. Which word best describes the Chorus' response to Medea's plan?
    A. thrilled
    B. indifferent
    C. confused
    D. horrified

11. What happens as Medea is murdering the children?
    A. Jason runs in and intervenes.
    B. Medea laughs and cries at the same time.
    C. The Chorus and the children briefly converse.
    D. Strange music is heard in the palace.

12. Which is best, according to the Chorus?
    A. exile
    B. passion
    C. moderation
    D. mercy

III. Quotations: Explain the importance and meaning of the following quotations:

1. This is the greatest salvation,
   when a wife stands together with her husband.
   But, now it's all hate, what was dearest is sick,
   for Jason betrayed his children and my mistress
   and goes to bed with a royal marriage.

2. But go inside now and bring her out
   of the house. Tell her we come as friends,
   make haste before she does something bad
   to those within, for this sorrow will set something
   great in motion.

3. This is not the first time that I've said it,
   but harsh anger is an unbearable evil.

4. Let no one think me
   weak or helpless or calm, but the other sort,
   hard on enemies and kind to friends.

5. Yes, by the gods, stop it! The time is critical!

IV. Vocabulary

____ 1. REBUKE   A. rebellious
____ 2. CONTUMACIOUS   B. to use
____ 3. MODERATION   C. lacking respect for religion
____ 4. DICTATORIAL   D. someone who pleads
____ 5. WIELD   E. related to marriage
____ 6. NUPTIAL   F. hatred
____ 7. SUPPLIANT   G. balance
____ 8. IMPIOUS   H. to criticize
____ 9. BENEFACTOR   I. a helper
____ 10. BILE   J. bossy

V. Composition
1. What is the climax of the play? Be sure to support your answer.

2. What persuasive techniques does Medea use in the play? Consider at least two instances of persuasion, and explain how they might contribute to the plot, characterization, and themes of the play.

Medea Multiple Choice Unit Test 2 Answer Key

I. Matching

A	1.	MEDEA	A.	murders her children, the princess, and Creon
F	2.	COLCHIS	B.	king of the Gods; Medea prays to him.
E	3.	ARGO	C.	pull Medea's chariot
D	4.	CHILDREN	D.	take gifts to the princess; murdered by Medea
B	5.	ZEUS	E.	Jason's ship
G	6.	PRINCESS	F.	Medea's hometown
C	7.	DRAGONS	G.	Jason's second wife; she dies from a poisoned dress.

II. Multiple Choice

A 1.   What was the name of Jason's ship?
   A. the *Argo*
   B. the *Mighty Jason*
   C. the *Golden Fleece*
   D. the *Bounty*

C 2.   What happened to Pelias, and who was responsible for it?
   A. Medea poisoned him.
   B. Jason killed him in battle.
   C. Medea tricked Pelias' daughters into killing him.
   D. He died of natural causes; no one was responsible.

B 3.   What bad news does the Tutor bring to the nurse?
   A. Creon has decided that the children no longer need a nurse.
   B. Medea and her children have been exiled from Corinth.
   C. Jason has decided to marry Creon's daughter.
   D. Medea is unhappy in Corinth and wants to go home.

B 4.   What does the Nurse say about power?
   A. Power is good for men, but not for women.
   B. Power is dangerous and can cause harm.
   C. People like power and should have it.
   D. People abuse power, but should still have it.

B 5.   Why does Creon exile Medea?
   A. He has been told to do so by the oracle.
   B. He fears that she will harm him or his family.
   C. He thinks she is someone else.
   D. He does not like Jason.

A 6.   What does Medea do to try to persuade Creon to let her stay?
   A. She embraces Creon's knees.
   B. She prays to Zeus.
   C. She gives him a gold crown.
   D. She offers him her children.

C 7. Why does Creon allow Medea to stay in the country for one day?
- A. He will be leaving Corinth in one day.
- B. He needs her to make a potion for him.
- C. He reasons that Medea cannot do anything terrible in one day.
- D. He wants to get back at his daughter for marrying Jason.

B 8. Which of the following is NOT something Medea did for Jason, according to the speech she makes?
- A. She betrayed her father in order to marry Jason.
- B. She allowed Jason to divorce her and marry Creon's daughter.
- C. She helped Jason kill the dragon that was guarding the Golden Fleece.
- D. She had Pelias brutally murdered.

C 9. What does Medea make Aegeus promise to do?
- A. adopt her children
- B. talk to Creon for her
- C. give her safe harbor
- D. leave her all his money

D 10. Which word best describes the Chorus' response to Medea's plan?
- A. thrilled
- B. indifferent
- C. confused
- D. horrified

C 11. What happens as Medea is murdering the children?
- A. Jason runs in and intervenes.
- B. Medea laughs and cries at the same time.
- C. The Chorus and the children briefly converse.
- D. Strange music is heard in the palace.

C 12. Which is best, according to the Chorus?
- A. exile
- B. passion
- C. moderation
- D. mercy

IV. Vocabulary

H	1. REBUKE	A.	rebellious
A	2. CONTUMACIOUS	B.	to use
G	3. MODERATION	C.	lacking respect for religion
J	4. DICTATORIAL	D.	someone who pleads
B	5. WIELD	E.	related to marriage
E	6. NUPTIAL	F.	hatred
D	7. SUPPLIANT	G.	balance
C	8. IMPIOUS	H.	to criticize
I	9. BENEFACTOR	I.	a helper
F	10. BILE	J.	bossy

UNIT RESOURCE MATERIALS

BULLETIN BOARD IDEAS *Medea*

1. Divide the class into groups, and have each group draw and cut out one of the following:

   skene
   orchestra
   proskenion
   theatron

   Then, put the parts together on the bulletin board to form an ancient Greek theater.

2. Write down and cut out the words, punctuation marks, and letters from Group A and put them on the board in random order. Then, cut out the words from Group B and put them in a separate group on the board. As a class, form a sentence that explains what each of the items in Group B is or does. In addition, try to make sentences that explain how the items are related. For example, one sentence might be, "The Chorus is a group that sings." You could also have, "The Chorus sings the ode."

   Group A

   in
   a
   an
   sing
   ,
   composed
   of
   the
   and
   s
   together
   is
   that
   during
   enter
   opening
   introduction
   story
   group

   Chorus
   Hero/Heroine
   Strophe
   Antistrophe
   Ode
   Epode
   Kommos
   Prologue
   Parodos

3. Write several of the most significant quotations from the play on the board on brightly colored paper.

4. List the vocabulary words for this unit. As you complete sections of the play and discuss the vocabulary for each section, write the definitions on the bulletin board. If your board is one that students face frequently, it will help them learn the words.

5. Make a map showing Greece, Corinth, the Black Sea, Colchis, the supposed location of the Symplegades, Iolcus, Pelion, and Athens. Cut out a boat and label it *Argo*. Using the boat, trace the journey of Medea and Jason, and give each place a short label. For example, for "Pelion," you could write, "Mountain where the *Argo* was built."

6. Divide the class into four or five groups, and give each group a section of the play. On the bulletin board, create two columns: "Greeks" and "Barbarians."
List the attributes you find in the play for each group under the different headings.

7. List all references to witchcraft that you can find in the play.

8. Make a column labeled "Men" and a column labeled "Women."
As a class, write down on pieces of paper the rights that each gender has according to the play. Put each piece of paper under the correct column.

9. Save one corner of the board for the best of students' *Medea* writing assignments.

10. List the different motivations characters have for their actions (money, revenge, safety, etc.). When students finish reading the play, have them pick out the motivation that they think is behind most actions that people take.

11. Pin up all the reasons a person might be considered an outsider in a society. Then, pin up some effects of being an outsider and some actions the person might take to adapt to society.

RELATED TOPICS *Medea*

1. Feminism
2. Tragedy
3. Ancient Greece
4. Mythology
5. Witchcraft
6. Exile
7. Homesickness
8. Alienation
9. Immigration
10. Drama

MORE ACTIVITIES *Medea*

1. Have students interpret the character of Medea artistically in ink, paint, sculpture, or another medium.
2. Have students design a playbill for *Medea*.
3. Have students design a bulletin board (ready to be put up; not just sketched) for *Medea*.
4. Use the Internet to look up cases in which a person took revenge after being spurned by a lover or spouse.
5. Discuss recent horror films that portray elements of witchcraft. Who is practicing witchcraft in the film, and what does this say about the character? Is witchcraft presented positively or negatively?
6. Create a lesson around the subjects of alienation and loneliness. Discuss reasons a person might feel alienated and the things a person might do in response. Ask for volunteers to describe times they felt like outsiders and what they did about it. Have them also give some examples of times when they left someone else out. Are there stories in the news about people doing things because they feel alienated?
7. Create a lesson around the idea of compromise. Use the following questions as a starting point:
   If you were Medea, would you carry out your plan for revenge?
   Could anything make Medea forgive Jason?
   Do you see any problems with Jason's justification for his actions?
   When is compromise necessary? When is it the wrong thing to do?
8. Look for stories in the news about gender discrimination and discuss them in relation to the play. Divide the class into two teams and debate the following point: Women are still limited by society. Be sure each team uses specific evidence to support its argument.
9. Stage *Medea* for other classes in your school.
10. Have students create a Venn Diagram for at least two of the main characters.

QUOTATIONS WORKSHEET *Medea*

1. This is the greatest salvation,
   when a wife stands together with her husband.
   But, now it's all hate, what was dearest is sick,
   for Jason betrayed his children and my mistress
   and goes to bed with a royal marriage.

2. Alas!
   I have suffered, oh, dreadfully
   have I suffered things
   worthy of lamentation.

3. But go inside now and bring her out
   of the house. Tell her we come as friends,
   make haste before she does something bad
   to those within, for this sorrow will set something
   great in motion.

4. Of all things that live and have intelligence,
   we women are the most wretched creatures.

5. I...am alone, without city, carried off from a barbarian land, with no mother, no
   brother, no relative to whom I could sail, away from this disaster.

6. ...I declare that you must leave
   this land in exile, taking your two children
   with you, and don't delay at all.

7. Do you think I would flatter that man
   if I had no plan or profit in it?

8. The streams run up the holy rivers
   and justice and everything else is reversed...

9. This is not the first time that I've said it,
   but harsh anger is an unbearable evil.

10. I saved you, as all the Greeks know who sailed
    with you on your ship, the Argo.

11. ...I call the gods to witness how I
    would do anything to help you and the children,
    but good things don't please you.

12. O fatherland, O home, never let me be
    without my city,
    leading a life of impossibility, difficult
    to endure, the most pitiful of pains.

13. This is how it is with me: When you come
    to my land, I will try to help you with
    justice on my side.

14. I shall send them bearing gifts to her,
    a delicate dress and golden crown.

15. Let no one think me
    weak or helpless or calm, but the other sort,
    hard on enemies and kind to friends.

16. Since you shared your plan with us, I want to
    help you and aid the laws of humanity:
    please don't do this.

17. I seek pardon and agree that
    I spoke badly then, but I've rethought it all now.

18. And you, wretched man, disastrously
    married to royal kin,
    unknowingly, you are bringing
    mortal destruction to your sons and
    hateful death to your wife.
    Poor man, how much you misunderstand your destiny.

19. Cheer up! You'll return soon, through your sons'
    influence.

20. O dearest hands! and dearest mouths and shape
    and beautiful face of my children!

21. I myself with happiness
    followed the boys to the women's quarters.

22. Come, wretched hand of mine, take the sword.

23. Pollution from relatives is difficult for mortals,
    and it brings grief to kinslayers in tune with
    their crime, falling on their house by god's will.

24. Should I go into the house? I think I should stop the murder for the children.

25. Yes, by the gods, stop it! The time is critical!

26. Loose the bolts as quickly as you can, servants,
    open the doors, let me see this double evil,
    them dead and her...I'll make her pay for it.

27. My grandfather
    the Sun is giving me this chariot,
    for protection against hostile hands.

28. Allow me to bury and mourn these corpses.

UNIT WORD LIST *Medea*

No.	Word	Clue/Definition
1.	AEGEUS	king of Athens; promises Medea safe harbor
2.	ARGO	Jason's ship
3.	ATHENS	Medea plans to flee to this city of wisdom and harmony.
4.	CHILDREN	take gifts to the princess; murdered by Medea
5.	CHORAGOS	the leader of the Chorus
6.	CHORUS	a group of characters that acts as one
7.	COLCHIS	Medea's hometown
8.	CORINTH	the town where Medea lives
9.	CREON	king of Corinth; father of the princess
10.	DRAGONS	pull Medea's chariot
11.	EKKYKLEMA	a wheeled cart on which dead bodies are usually brought out
12.	EPISODE	spoken lines; takes place between odes
13.	EXODUS	the final scene of dialogue
14.	JASON	Medea's unfaithful husband
15.	MEDEA	murders her children, the princess, and Creon
16.	MESSENGER	tells Medea about the deaths of the princess and Creon and advises her to flee immediately
17.	NURSE	Medea's servant; wants a life of moderation
18.	ORACLE	the holy place where Aegeus goes to receive advice from the gods
19.	ORCHESTRA	the area in front of the stage where the Chorus dances
20.	PARODOS	the first entrance of the Chorus
21.	PELIAS	murdered by his own daughters
22.	PHOEBUS	didn't give women music—they might sing about the badness of men.
23.	PITTHEUS	King of Troezen; Aegeus wants to consult him.
24.	PRINCESS	Jason's second wife; she dies from a poisoned dress.
25.	PROLOGUE	the part of the play before the Chorus enters
26.	SKENE	the actors enter and exit the stage through this.
27.	STASIMON	Greek term for ode; takes place between dramatic episodes
28.	THEATRON	the area from which the audience watches the action
29.	TUTOR	tells the Nurse about Medea's exile
30.	ZEUS	king of the Gods; Medea prays to him.

WORD SEARCH Medea

```
T O R C H E S T R A E M E D E A X W M N
H P N Y K H X Z Z S P E N Y S W W T N L
E B N T L N L R C T I S N D M R M Y X B
A W Y T C Z M T A S S N B F R N C B B
T H P I T T H E U S O E W N L Y J C Y H
R J S K N Q W L C I D N Q M H H X L B S
O K S S M X C Z C M E G W T V L T P F G
N X F N N F G H K O N E R N N H R Z F Y
K J F O J E C H O N X R W C B O B N R R
G T J R Y X T G T R V S O N L Z E F G P
P U A A Z O H F C B A L P O P R Y S O V
Y T S C E D P H O N C G G H D C K A G D
P O O L U U D R R H K U O L O R M M R B
P R N E S S S A I L E P I S K E N E A M
L A Q U U W E S N N P H N Z L O B T N Q
V Y R R R G X F T B C O C K J N H U M C
B B O O E S L N H H G E Y R N E P Z S D
Q H N U D N E Z T A B K S K N X G G F K
C G S X M O W W R M K S N S W F V P Z W
M D Y Q N J S D G E S C Y J X K N Q R Q
```

AEGEUS	CREON	NURSE	PROLOGUE
ARGO	DRAGONS	ORACLE	SKENE
ATHENS	EKKYKLEMA	ORCHESTRA	STASIMON
CHILDREN	EPISODE	PARODOS	THEATRON
CHORAGOS	EXODUS	PELIAS	TUTOR
CHORUS	JASON	PHOEBUS	ZEUS
COLCHIS	MEDEA	PITTHEUS	
CORINTH	MESSENGER	PRINCESS	

WORD SEARCH ANSWER KEY Medea

```
T   O R C H E S T R A E M E D E A
H                   S P   E
E                   T I   S
A                   A S   S
T     P I T T H E U S O   E
R                   I D   N                       P
O             C     M E   G                       R
N           H       O     E                       O
          O     E       O   R     C       O       L
      T J R     X       R         O       L       O
      U A A Z           C     A   P       R       G
      T S C E D     P   O     C G G H D C         U
      O O L U   U     R R H   U O L   R M       A E
    P R N E S   S A   I L E   P I S   K E     N R
      A   U U     E S N       H N     L O     B T
          R R G       T       C       K N     H U
          O O E       S       H       G E     U
        H   U D       E       A       K S     N S
      C     S         O       R       K       S
                      S D     E
```

AEGEUS
ARGO
ATHENS
CHILDREN
CHORAGOS
CHORUS
COLCHIS
CORINTH

CREON
DRAGONS
EKKYKLEMA
EPISODE
EXODUS
JASON
MEDEA
MESSENGER

NURSE
ORACLE
ORCHESTRA
PARODOS
PELIAS
PHOEBUS
PITTHEUS
PRINCESS

PROLOGUE
SKENE
STASIMON
THEATRON
TUTOR
ZEUS

CROSSWORD Medea

Across
3. the holy place where Aegeus goes to receive advice from the gods
5. spoken lines; takes place between odes
7. tells the Nurse about Medea's exile
8. the leader of the Chorus
10. king of Athens; promises Medea safe harbor
11. Medea's servant; wants a life of moderation
12. Jason's ship
14. Medea's unfaithful husband
16. Medea plans to flee to this city of wisdom and harmony
19. a group of characters that acts as one
20. king of Corinth; father of the princess
21. king of the Gods; Medea prays to him
22. Jason's second wife; she dies from a poisoned dress

Down
1. King of Troezen; Aegeus wants to consult him
2. Greek term for ode; takes place between dramatic episodes
3. the area in front of the stage where the Chorus dances
4. the town where Medea lives
5. a wheeled cart on which dead bodies are usually brought out
6. pull Medea's chariot
7. the area from which the audience watches the action
9. the actors enter and exit the stage through this
13. Medea's hometown
15. the first entrance of the Chorus
17. the final scene of dialogue
18. murders her children, the princess, and Creon

CROSSWORD ANSWER KEY Medea

Across
3. the holy place where Aegeus goes to receive advice from the gods
5. spoken lines; takes place between odes
7. tells the Nurse about Medea's exile
8. the leader of the Chorus
10. king of Athens; promises Medea safe harbor
11. Medea's servant; wants a life of moderation
12. Jason's ship
14. Medea's unfaithful husband
16. Medea plans to flee to this city of wisdom and harmony
19. a group of characters that acts as one
20. king of Corinth; father of the princess
21. king of the Gods; Medea prays to him
22. Jason's second wife; she dies from a poisoned dress

Down
1. King of Troezen; Aegeus wants to consult him
2. Greek term for ode; takes place between dramatic episodes
3. the area in front of the stage where the Chorus dances
4. the town where Medea lives
5. a wheeled cart on which dead bodies are usually brought out
6. pull Medea's chariot
7. the area from which the audience watches the action
9. the actors enter and exit the stage through this
13. Medea's hometown
15. the first entrance of the Chorus
17. the final scene of dialogue
18. murders her children, the princess, and Creon

MATCHING 1 *Medea*

___ 1. EPISODE   A. king of Corinth; father of the princess
___ 2. JASON   B. the final scene of dialogue
___ 3. ORACLE   C. murders her children, the princess, and Creon
___ 4. PITTHEUS   D. a group of characters that acts as one
___ 5. PROLOGUE   E. Jason's second wife; she dies from a poisoned dress.
___ 6. EKKYKLEMA   F. the part of the play before the Chorus enters
___ 7. EXODUS   G. Medea's unfaithful husband
___ 8. CHORAGOS   H. the town where Medea lives
___ 9. STASIMON   I. Medea's servant; wants a life of moderation
___ 10. MEDEA   J. Jason's ship
___ 11. CORINTH   K. Greek term for ode; takes place between dramatic episodes
___ 12. NURSE   L. the leader of the Chorus
___ 13. PRINCESS   M. king of the Gods; Medea prays to him.
___ 14. ZEUS   N. take gifts to the princess; murdered by Medea
___ 15. CHILDREN   O. tells the Nurse about Medea's exile
___ 16. CREON   P. spoken lines; takes place between odes
___ 17. CHORUS   Q. didn't give women music—they might sing about the badness of men.
___ 18. TUTOR   R. the holy place where Aegeus goes to receive advice from the gods
___ 19. ARGO   S. King of Troezen; Aegeus wants to consult him.
___ 20. PHOEBUS   T. a wheeled cart on which dead bodies are usually brought out

MATCHING 1 ANSWER KEY *Medea*

P	1.	EPISODE	A.	king of Corinth; father of the princess
G	2.	JASON	B.	the final scene of dialogue
R	3.	ORACLE	C.	murders her children, the princess, and Creon
S	4.	PITTHEUS	D.	a group of characters that acts as one
F	5.	PROLOGUE	E.	Jason's second wife; she dies from a poisoned dress.
T	6.	EKKYKLEMA	F.	the part of the play before the Chorus enters
B	7.	EXODUS	G.	Medea's unfaithful husband
L	8.	CHORAGOS	H.	the town where Medea lives
K	9.	STASIMON	I.	Medea's servant; wants a life of moderation
C	10.	MEDEA	J.	Jason's ship
H	11.	CORINTH	K.	Greek term for ode; takes place between dramatic episodes
I	12.	NURSE	L.	the leader of the Chorus
E	13.	PRINCESS	M.	king of the Gods; Medea prays to him.
M	14.	ZEUS	N.	take gifts to the princess; murdered by Medea
N	15.	CHILDREN	O.	tells the Nurse about Medea's exile
A	16.	CREON	P.	spoken lines; takes place between odes
D	17.	CHORUS	Q.	didn't give women music—they might sing about the badness of men.
O	18.	TUTOR	R.	the holy place where Aegeus goes to receive advice from the gods
J	19.	ARGO	S.	King of Troezen; Aegeus wants to consult him.
Q	20.	PHOEBUS	T.	a wheeled cart on which dead bodies are usually brought out

MATCHING 2 *Medea*

____ 1. PITTHEUS   A. the area in front of the stage where the Chorus dances

____ 2. MESSENGER   B. Medea plans to flee to this city of wisdom and harmony.

____ 3. ATHENS   C. Medea's unfaithful husband

____ 4. THEATRON   D. king of Corinth; father of the princess

____ 5. ORCHESTRA   E. king of the Gods; Medea prays to him.

____ 6. CHORAGOS   F. a group of characters that acts as one

____ 7. SKENE   G. pull Medea's chariot

____ 8. PARODOS   H. King of Troezen; Aegeus wants to consult him.

____ 9. STASIMON   I. the first entrance of the Chorus

____ 10. CORINTH   J. Medea's hometown

____ 11. COLCHIS   K. didn't give women music—they might sing about the badness of men.

____ 12. JASON   L. the area from which the audience watches the action

____ 13. DRAGONS   M. the actors enter and exit the stage through this.

____ 14. ZEUS   N. murdered by his own daughters

____ 15. AEGEUS   O. the town where Medea lives

____ 16. CHILDREN   P. the leader of the Chorus

____ 17. CREON   Q. king of Athens; promises Medea safe harbor

____ 18. CHORUS   R. take gifts to the princess; murdered by Medea

____ 19. PELIAS   S. tells Medea about the deaths of the princess and Creon and advises her to flee immediately

____ 20. PHOEBUS   T. Greek term for ode; takes place between dramatic episodes

MATCHING 2 ANSWER KEY *Medea*

H	1.	PITTHEUS	A.	the area in front of the stage where the Chorus dances
S	2.	MESSENGER	B.	Medea plans to flee to this city of wisdom and harmony.
B	3.	ATHENS	C.	Medea's unfaithful husband
L	4.	THEATRON	D.	king of Corinth; father of the princess
A	5.	ORCHESTRA	E.	king of the Gods; Medea prays to him.
P	6.	CHORAGOS	F.	a group of characters that acts as one
M	7.	SKENE	G.	pull Medea's chariot
I	8.	PARODOS	H.	King of Troezen; Aegeus wants to consult him.
T	9.	STASIMON	I.	the first entrance of the Chorus
O	10.	CORINTH	J.	Medea's hometown
J	11.	COLCHIS	K.	didn't give women music—they might sing about the badness of men.
C	12.	JASON	L.	the area from which the audience watches the action
G	13.	DRAGONS	M.	the actors enter and exit the stage through this.
E	14.	ZEUS	N.	murdered by his own daughters
Q	15.	AEGEUS	O.	the town where Medea lives
R	16.	CHILDREN	P.	the leader of the Chorus
D	17.	CREON	Q.	king of Athens; promises Medea safe harbor
F	18.	CHORUS	R.	take gifts to the princess; murdered by Medea
N	19.	PELIAS	S.	tells Medea about the deaths of the princess and Creon and advises her to flee immediately
K	20.	PHOEBUS	T.	Greek term for ode; takes place between dramatic episodes

JUGGLE LETTERS 1 *Medea*

_____ = 1. EEIDOSP
spoken lines; takes place between odes

_____ = 2. NASOJ
Medea's unfaithful husband

_____ = 3. ALCEOR
the holy place where Aegeus goes to receive advice from the gods

_____ = 4. OLUPOGRE
the part of the play before the Chorus enters

_____ = 5. RNOTHTEA
the area from which the audience watches the action

_____ = 6. EKKAKMELY
a wheeled cart on which dead bodies are usually brought out

_____ = 7. RTOCREHSA
the area in front of the stage where the Chorus dances

_____ = 8. ACSHOROG
the leader of the Chorus

_____ = 9. DAPORSO
the first entrance of the Chorus

_____ = 10. EDAME
murders her children, the princess, and Creon

_____ = 11. IORTNHC
the town where Medea lives

_____ = 12. SUNRE
Medea's servant; wants a life of moderation

_____ = 13. NPIRESSC
Jason's second wife; she dies from a poisoned dress.

_____ = 14. UEZS
king of the Gods; Medea prays to him.

_____ = 15. UGEEAS
king of Athens; promises Medea safe harbor

_____ = 16. HDRENLIC
take gifts to the princess; murdered by Medea

_____ = 17. HSOCRU
a group of characters that acts as one

_____ = 18. TTORU
tells the Nurse about Medea's exile

_____ = 19. GRAO
Jason's ship

_____ = 20. TMNISSAO
Greek term for ode; takes place between dramatic episodes

JUGGLE LETTERS 1 ANSWER KEY *Medea*

EPISODE	= 1.	EEIDOSP
		spoken lines; takes place between odes
JASON	= 2.	NASOJ
		Medea's unfaithful husband
ORACLE	= 3.	ALCEOR
		the holy place where Aegeus goes to receive advice from the gods
PROLOGUE	= 4.	OLUPOGRE
		the part of the play before the Chorus enters
THEATRON	= 5.	RNOTHTEA
		the area from which the audience watches the action
EKKYKLEMA	= 6.	EKKAKMELY
		a wheeled cart on which dead bodies are usually brought out
ORCHESTRA	= 7.	RTOCREHSA
		the area in front of the stage where the Chorus dances
CHORAGOS	= 8.	ACSHOROG
		the leader of the Chorus
PARODOS	= 9.	DAPORSO
		the first entrance of the Chorus
MEDEA	= 10.	EDAME
		murders her children, the princess, and Creon
CORINTH	= 11.	IORTNHC
		the town where Medea lives
NURSE	= 12.	SUNRE
		Medea's servant; wants a life of moderation
PRINCESS	= 13.	NPIRESSC
		Jason's second wife; she dies from a poisoned dress.
ZEUS	= 14.	UEZS
		king of the Gods; Medea prays to him.
AEGEUS	= 15.	UGEEAS
		king of Athens; promises Medea safe harbor
CHILDREN	= 16.	HDRENLIC
		take gifts to the princess; murdered by Medea
CHORUS	= 17.	HSOCRU
		a group of characters that acts as one
TUTOR	= 18.	TTORU
		tells the Nurse about Medea's exile
ARGO	= 19.	GRAO
		Jason's ship
STASIMON	= 20.	TMNISSAO
		Greek term for ode; takes place between dramatic episodes

JUGGLE LETTERS 2 *Medea*

_____ = 1. SOGADNR
pull Medea's chariot

_____ = 2. SAONJ
Medea's unfaithful husband

_____ = 3. IUSEHTTP
King of Troezen; Aegeus wants to consult him.

_____ = 4. GMESENESR
tells Medea about the deaths of the princess and Creon and advises her to flee immediately

_____ = 5. EHNTAS
Medea plans to flee to this city of wisdom and harmony.

_____ = 6. EOUSXD
the final scene of dialogue

_____ = 7. ARHCREOTS
the area in front of the stage where the Chorus dances

_____ = 8. OGORSHAC
the leader of the Chorus

_____ = 9. SPAODOR
the first entrance of the Chorus

_____ = 10. EMEDA
murders her children, the princess, and Creon

_____ = 11. ICNROHT
the town where Medea lives

_____ = 12. PNIECSSR
Jason's second wife; she dies from a poisoned dress.

_____ = 13. EZUS
king of the Gods; Medea prays to him.

_____ = 14. GEUESA
king of Athens; promises Medea safe harbor

_____ = 15. CIEDNLHR
take gifts to the princess; murdered by Medea

_____ = 16. NCROE
king of Corinth; father of the princess

_____ = 17. HOCRSU
a group of characters that acts as one

_____ = 18. PEIALS
murdered by his own daughters

_____ = 19. LICOSHC
Medea's hometown

_____ = 20. HOUPBSE
didn't give women music—they might sing about the badness of men.

JUGGLE LETTERS 2 ANSWER KEY *Medea*

DRAGONS	= 1.	SOGADNR
		pull Medea's chariot
JASON	= 2.	SAONJ
		Medea's unfaithful husband
PITTHEUS	= 3.	IUSEHTTP
		King of Troezen; Aegeus wants to consult him.
MESSENGER	= 4.	GMESENESR
		tells Medea about the deaths of the princess and Creon and advises her to flee immediately
ATHENS	= 5.	EHNTAS
		Medea plans to flee to this city of wisdom and harmony.
EXODUS	= 6.	EOUSXD
		the final scene of dialogue
ORCHESTRA	= 7.	ARHCREOTS
		the area in front of the stage where the Chorus dances
CHORAGOS	= 8.	OGORSHAC
		the leader of the Chorus
PARODOS	= 9.	SPAODOR
		the first entrance of the Chorus
MEDEA	= 10.	EMEDA
		murders her children, the princess, and Creon
CORINTH	= 11.	ICNROHT
		the town where Medea lives
PRINCESS	= 12.	PNIECSSR
		Jason's second wife; she dies from a poisoned dress.
ZEUS	= 13.	EZUS
		king of the Gods; Medea prays to him.
AEGEUS	= 14.	GEUESA
		king of Athens; promises Medea safe harbor
CHILDREN	= 15.	CIEDNLHR
		take gifts to the princess; murdered by Medea
CREON	= 16.	NCROE
		king of Corinth; father of the princess
CHORUS	= 17.	HOCRSU
		a group of characters that acts as one
PELIAS	= 18.	PEIALS
		murdered by his own daughters
COLCHIS	= 19.	LICOSHC
		Medea's hometown
PHOEBUS	= 20.	HOUPBSE
		didn't give women music—they might sing about the badness of men.

VOCABULARY RESOURCE MATERIALS

Medea Vocabulary

No.	Word	Clue/Definition
1.	ABSTRUSE	hard to understand
2.	BARBARIAN	savage
3.	BASE	low; evil
4.	BASTION	a strong place
5.	BENEFACTOR	a helper
6.	BEREFT	without, lacking
7.	BILE	hatred
8.	COMPLEXION	coloring
9.	COMPREHENSION	understanding
10.	CONCESSIONS	allowances
11.	CONSORT	a mate, especially one outside of marriage
12.	CONTUMACIOUS	rebellious
13.	DICTATORIAL	bossy
14.	DOWRY	a bridal price
15.	ENJOIN	to command; order
16.	ENTREAT	to ask
17.	EXILE	an outcast
18.	EXPIATION	repayment for a wrong
19.	GARB	clothing
20.	GARLAND	a wreath
21.	HAVEN	a safe place
22.	HINDERING	stopping
23.	IMPIOUS	lacking respect for religion
24.	INCUR	to cause; invite
25.	INHOSPITABLE	unfriendly
26.	LAMENTATION	mourning
27.	LYRE	a stringed instrument
28.	MODERATION	balance
29.	MORTAL	a human
30.	NUPTIAL	related to marriage
31.	PEERLESS	unmatched
32.	PROMONTORY	a cliff
33.	PRUDENT	sensible
34.	RASH	careless; foolish
35.	REBUKE	to criticize
36.	REPROACH	to scold
37.	RESOLVE	determination
38.	SIRED	fathered
39.	SUPPLIANT	someone who pleads

No.	Word	Clue/Definition
40.	WIELD	to use
41.	WRATH	anger

VOCABULARY WORD SEARCH - Medea

```
C O N T U M A C I O U S T H E R A B C D
H Y R O T N O M O R P N V L D J B E O I
M N X K L N L Z Q M A X B P Q K S N M C
G B X B S A B H R I P A X T M G T E P T
D S U O I P M I L Y T L B H S A R F R A
Q X R T S N X P T I A H E A R D U A E T
X T P S E W P H P T D W I X S P S C H O
Z U H V L U G S R G N Q R N I E E T E R
N X A H S L O O W K A G C A D O G O N I
C H P X J H M N M Y L R B R T E N R S A
O S E Z N M G S T W R L B W R H R S I L
N J E I B Q E X P I A T I O N C C I O B
C H R D A C Q H R T G Q T A Q W V H N D
E R L B S N F V A W D W I K V T C H F G
S Q E L T L T E R C B R B R N A H L R G
S F S S I Y R P S E A S Y E O Q F U E W
I S S V O T K G I B B R D R C T C L X B
O P N T N L L Y R E W U P H E N J O I N
N M J E M M V A E O R E K M I J H L L G
S T F E R E B E D P R W I E L D E H E C
```

ABSTRUSE	CONSORT	HAVEN	PRUDENT
BARBARIAN	CONTUMACIOUS	HINDERING	RASH
BASE	DICTATORIAL	IMPIOUS	REBUKE
BASTION	DOWRY	INCUR	REPROACH
BENEFACTOR	ENJOIN	INHOSPITABLE	RESOLVE
BEREFT	ENTREAT	LYRE	SIRED
BILE	EXILE	MORTAL	SUPPLIANT
COMPLEXION	EXPIATION	NUPTIAL	WIELD
COMPREHENSION	GARB	PEERLESS	WRATH
CONCESSIONS	GARLAND	PROMONTORY	

VOCABULARY WORD SEARCH ANSWER KEY - Medea

```
C O N T U M A C I O U S T     E     A B C D
  Y R O T N O M O R P N   L       B E O I
        N L     M A   B         S N M C
        S A     I P A           T E P T
   S U O I P M I L   T L B H S A R F R A
    R T   N   P   I A H E A   U A E   T
   T P   E   P   P T D W I X S S C H   O
   U   V   U   S R G N   R N I E E T   R
 N   A   S     O O       A   A D O     I
 C H   P     H M         L   R   T E N R A
 O   E     N             R   B     H R   L
 N   E I B   E X P I A T I O N     I O
 C   R   A       T G     A         H N
 E R L   S     A         I       T     G
 S   E   T     E R       R       N A   R
 S   S S   R     S E A   Y E O     U E
 I   S     O T   I B   B R D R       C X B
 O       N   L Y R E W   U P   E N J O I N
 N         E     V A E O R E K   I     L
 S T F E R E B E D P R W I E L D E     E
```

ABSTRUSE
BARBARIAN
BASE
BASTION
BENEFACTOR
BEREFT
BILE
COMPLEXION
COMPREHENSION
CONCESSIONS

CONSORT
CONTUMACIOUS
DICTATORIAL
DOWRY
ENJOIN
ENTREAT
EXILE
EXPIATION
GARB
GARLAND

HAVEN
HINDERING
IMPIOUS
INCUR
INHOSPITABLE
LYRE
MORTAL
NUPTIAL
PEERLESS
PROMONTORY

PRUDENT
RASH
REBUKE
REPROACH
RESOLVE
SIRED
SUPPLIANT
WIELD
WRATH

VOCABULARY CROSSWORD - Medea

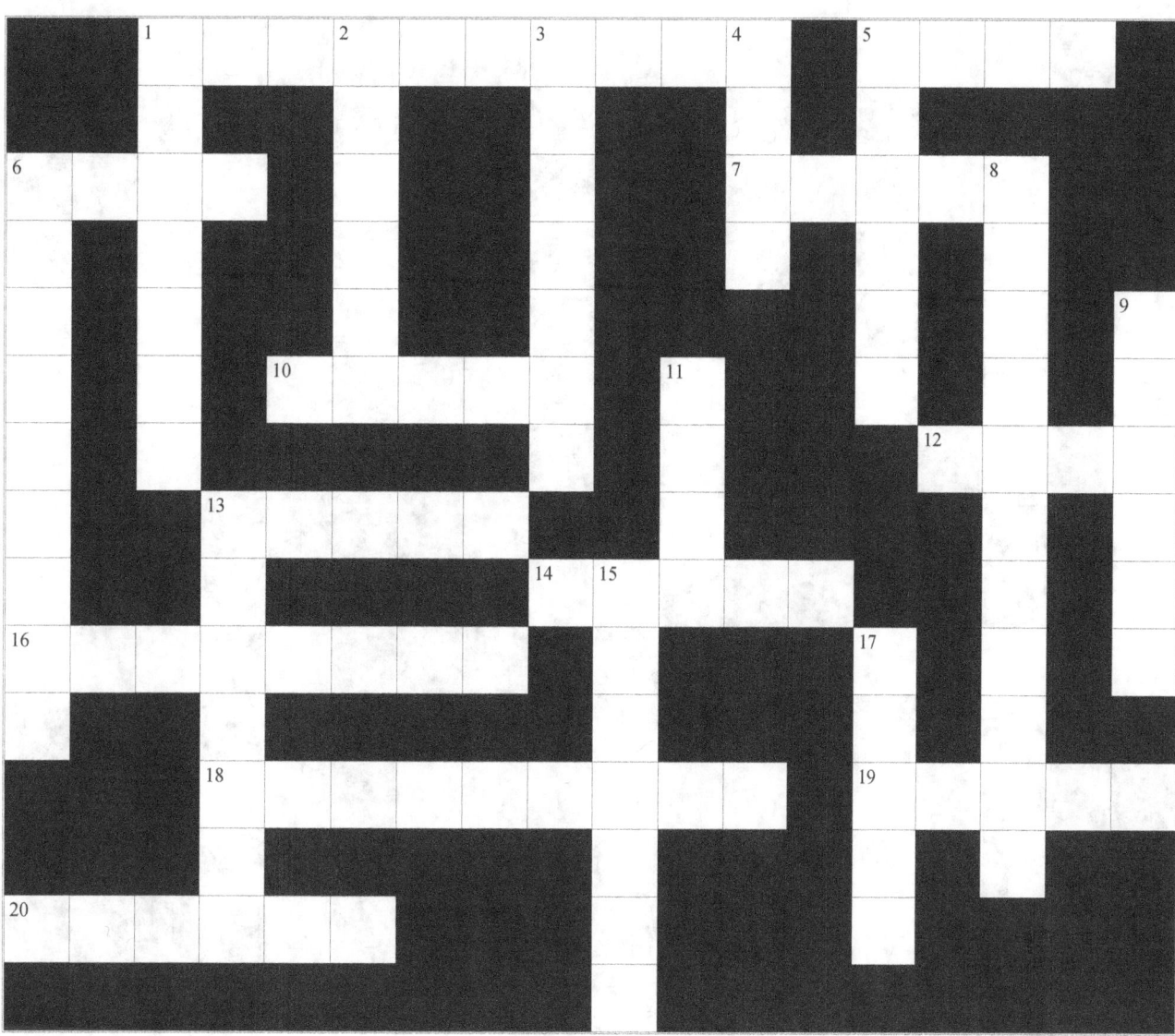

Across
1. a helper
5. hatred
6. low; evil
7. fathered
10. to cause; invite
12. clothing
13. an outcast
14. to use
16. hard to understand
18. repayment for a wrong
19. anger
20. a human

Down
1. a strong place
2. to command; order
3. a mate, especially one outside of marriage
4. careless; foolish
5. without, lacking
6. savage
8. bossy
9. to criticize
11. a stringed instrument
13. to ask
15. lacking respect for religion
17. a bridal price

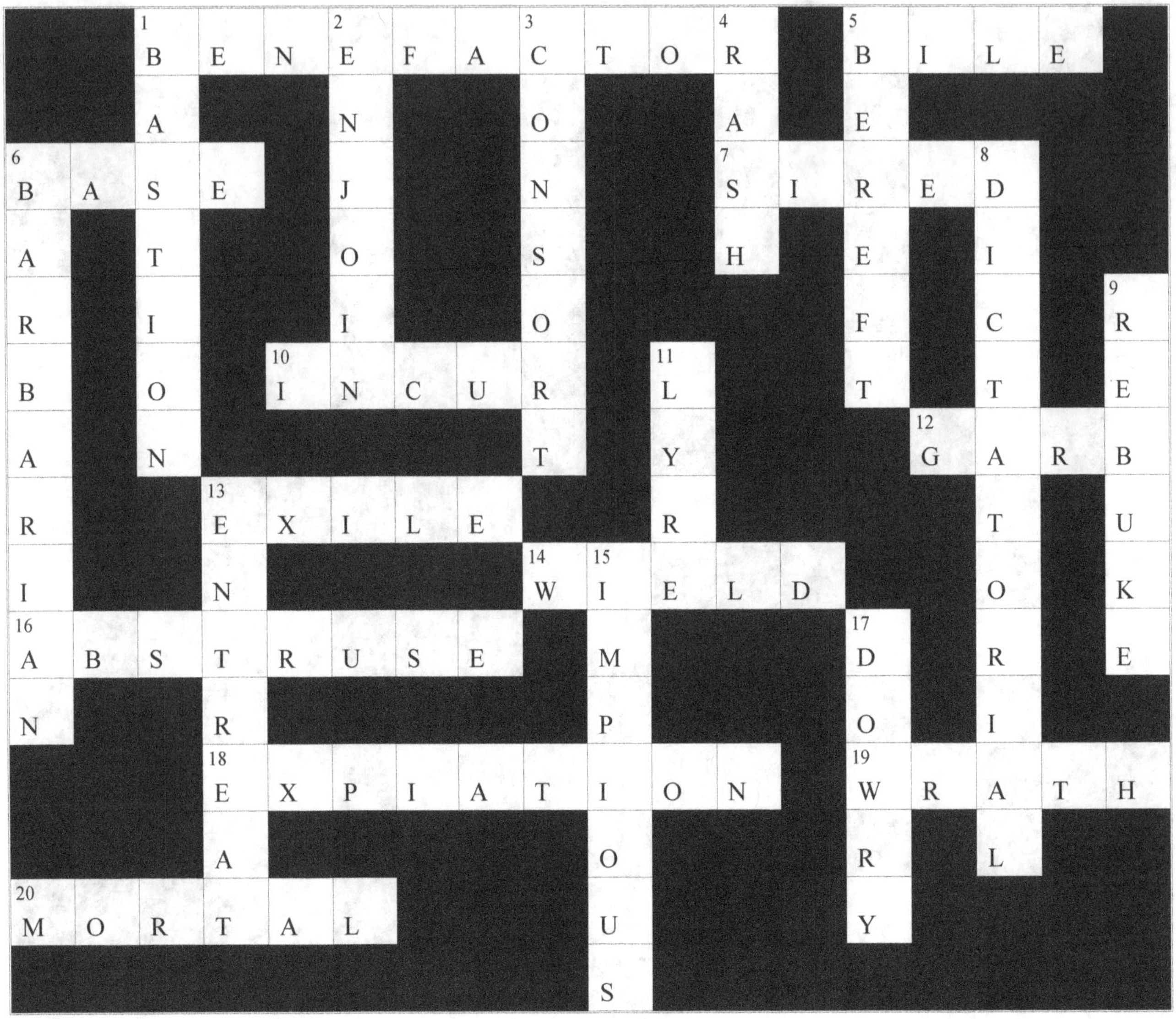

VOCABULARY CROSSWORD ANSWER KEY - Medea

Across
1. a helper
5. hatred
6. low; evil
7. fathered
10. to cause; invite
12. clothing
13. an outcast
14. to use
16. hard to understand
18. repayment for a wrong
19. anger
20. a human

Down
1. a strong place
2. to command; order
3. a mate, especially one outside of marriage
4. careless; foolish
5. without, lacking
6. savage
8. bossy
9. to criticize
11. a stringed instrument
13. to ask
15. lacking respect for religion
17. a bridal price

Answers Filled In

Across:
1. BENEFACTOR
5. BILE
6. BASE
7. SIRED
10. INCUR
12. GARB
13. EXILE
14. WIELD
16. ABSTRUSE
18. EXPIATION
19. WRATH
20. MORTAL

Down:
1. BASTION
2. ENJOIN
3. CONSORT
4. RASH
5. BEREFT
6. BARBARIAN
8. DICTATORIAL
9. REBUKE
11. LYRE
13. ENTREAT
15. IMPIOUS
17. DOWRY

VOCABULARY MATCHING 1 *Medea*

____ 1. SIRED   A. sensible
____ 2. ENTREAT   B. fathered
____ 3. DOWRY   C. a stringed instrument
____ 4. CONTUMACIOUS   D. repayment for a wrong
____ 5. CONCESSIONS   E. a wreath
____ 6. COMPLEXION   F. rebellious
____ 7. BEREFT   G. lacking respect for religion
____ 8. BASTION   H. without, lacking
____ 9. BARBARIAN   I. coloring
____ 10. EXPIATION   J. allowances
____ 11. GARLAND   K. to use
____ 12. REBUKE   L. unmatched
____ 13. PRUDENT   M. to criticize
____ 14. PEERLESS   N. a bridal price
____ 15. MORTAL   O. unfriendly
____ 16. LYRE   P. a safe place
____ 17. INHOSPITABLE Q. savage
____ 18. IMPIOUS   R. a strong place
____ 19. HAVEN   S. a human
____ 20. WIELD   T. to ask

VOCABULARY MATCHING 1 ANSWER KEY *Medea*

B	1.	SIRED	A.	sensible
T	2.	ENTREAT	B.	fathered
N	3.	DOWRY	C.	a stringed instrument
F	4.	CONTUMACIOUS	D.	repayment for a wrong
J	5.	CONCESSIONS	E.	a wreath
I	6.	COMPLEXION	F.	rebellious
H	7.	BEREFT	G.	lacking respect for religion
R	8.	BASTION	H.	without, lacking
Q	9.	BARBARIAN	I.	coloring
D	10.	EXPIATION	J.	allowances
E	11.	GARLAND	K.	to use
M	12.	REBUKE	L.	unmatched
A	13.	PRUDENT	M.	to criticize
L	14.	PEERLESS	N.	a bridal price
S	15.	MORTAL	O.	unfriendly
C	16.	LYRE	P.	a safe place
O	17.	INHOSPITABLE	Q.	savage
G	18.	IMPIOUS	R.	a strong place
P	19.	HAVEN	S.	a human
K	20.	WIELD	T.	to ask

VOCABULARY MATCHING 2 *Medea*

____ 1. SUPPLIANT   A. stopping
____ 2. ENJOIN   B. hard to understand
____ 3. DICTATORIAL   C. a helper
____ 4. CONSORT   D. balance
____ 5. COMPREHENSION   E. understanding
____ 6. BILE   F. to cause; invite
____ 7. BENEFACTOR   G. careless; foolish
____ 8. BASE   H. a mate, especially one outside of marriage
____ 9. ABSTRUSE   I. to command; order
____ 10. EXILE   J. anger
____ 11. GARLAND   K. hatred
____ 12. REPROACH   L. a cliff
____ 13. RASH   M. bossy
____ 14. PROMONTORY   N. someone who pleads
____ 15. NUPTIAL   O. a wreath
____ 16. MODERATION   P. low; evil
____ 17. LAMENTATION   Q. related to marriage
____ 18. INCUR   R. mourning
____ 19. HINDERING   S. an outcast
____ 20. WRATH   T. to scold

VOCABULARY MATCHING 2 ANSWER KEY *Medea*

N	1.	SUPPLIANT	A.	stopping
I	2.	ENJOIN	B.	hard to understand
M	3.	DICTATORIAL	C.	a helper
H	4.	CONSORT	D.	balance
E	5.	COMPREHENSION	E.	understanding
K	6.	BILE	F.	to cause; invite
C	7.	BENEFACTOR	G.	careless; foolish
P	8.	BASE	H.	a mate, especially one outside of marriage
B	9.	ABSTRUSE	I.	to command; order
S	10.	EXILE	J.	anger
O	11.	GARLAND	K.	hatred
T	12.	REPROACH	L.	a cliff
G	13.	RASH	M.	bossy
L	14.	PROMONTORY	N.	someone who pleads
Q	15.	NUPTIAL	O.	a wreath
D	16.	MODERATION	P.	low; evil
R	17.	LAMENTATION	Q.	related to marriage
F	18.	INCUR	R.	mourning
A	19.	HINDERING	S.	an outcast
J	20.	WRATH	T.	to scold

VOCABULARY JUGGLE LETTERS 1 *Medea*

_____ = 1. PUNTPALIS
someone who pleads

_____ = 2. NJNIEO
to command; order

_____ = 3. ICTOIALDATR
bossy

_____ = 4. ONTCRSO
a mate, especially one outside of marriage

_____ = 5. CNHNMRSPEIEOO
understanding

_____ = 6. IBEL
hatred

_____ = 7. EBEFATOCRN
a helper

_____ = 8. ABSE
low; evil

_____ = 9. ASRTBSEU
hard to understand

_____ = 10. IEXEL
an outcast

_____ = 11. RAAGLDN
a wreath

_____ = 12. RORAEPCH
to scold

_____ = 13. SHAR
careless; foolish

_____ = 14. TRMORPOYON
a cliff

_____ = 15. NTLIAUP
related to marriage

_____ = 16. AREIODONTM
balance

_____ = 17. IANMANTLEOT
mourning

_____ = 18. CURIN
to cause; invite

_____ = 19. GNRNIIEHD
stopping

_____ = 20. RTAHW
anger

VOCABULARY JUGGLE LETTERS 1 ANSWER KEY *Medea*

SUPPLIANT	= 1.	PUNTPALIS someone who pleads
ENJOIN	= 2.	NJNIEO to command; order
DICTATORIAL	= 3.	ICTOIALDATR bossy
CONSORT	= 4.	ONTCRSO a mate, especially one outside of marriage
COMPREHENSION	= 5.	CNHNMRSPEIEOO understanding
BILE	= 6.	IBEL hatred
BENEFACTOR	= 7.	EBEFATOCRN a helper
BASE	= 8.	ABSE low; evil
ABSTRUSE	= 9.	ASRTBSEU hard to understand
EXILE	= 10.	IEXEL an outcast
GARLAND	= 11.	RAAGLDN a wreath
REPROACH	= 12.	RORAEPCH to scold
RASH	= 13.	SHAR careless; foolish
PROMONTORY	= 14.	TRMORPOYON a cliff
NUPTIAL	= 15.	NTLIAUP related to marriage
MODERATION	= 16.	AREIODONTM balance
LAMENTATION	= 17.	IANMANTLEOT mourning
INCUR	= 18.	CURIN to cause; invite
HINDERING	= 19.	GNRNIIEHD stopping
WRATH	= 20.	RTAHW anger

VOCABULARY JUGGLE LETTERS 2 *Medea*

_____ = 1. ERISD
fathered

_____ = 2. RTENAET
to ask

_____ = 3. WRODY
a bridal price

_____ = 4. USAMCNCOUIOT
rebellious

_____ = 5. NOSSCESINOC
allowances

_____ = 6. OXEOPNMLIC
coloring

_____ = 7. ETFBER
without, lacking

_____ = 8. IOBSTNA
a strong place

_____ = 9. RNBRIAABA
savage

_____ = 10. EIXIATPNO
repayment for a wrong

_____ = 11. NAHVE
a safe place

_____ = 12. BEEUKR
to criticize

_____ = 13. PTUNDER
sensible

_____ = 14. LSRESEEP
unmatched

_____ = 15. MLRATO
a human

_____ = 16. TOMEDORNAI
balance

_____ = 17. RYLE
a stringed instrument

_____ = 18. AOLIPNTHBISE
unfriendly

_____ = 19. SIPIUMO
lacking respect for religion

_____ = 20. IDWEL
to use

VOCABULARY JUGGLE LETTERS 2 ANSWER KEY *Medea*

SIRED	= 1.	ERISD fathered
ENTREAT	= 2.	RTENAET to ask
DOWRY	= 3.	WRODY a bridal price
CONTUMACIOUS	= 4.	USAMCNCOUIOT rebellious
CONCESSIONS	= 5.	NOSSCESINOC allowances
COMPLEXION	= 6.	OXEOPNMLIC coloring
BEREFT	= 7.	ETFBER without, lacking
BASTION	= 8.	IOBSTNA a strong place
BARBARIAN	= 9.	RNBRIAABA savage
EXPIATION	= 10.	EIXIATPNO repayment for a wrong
HAVEN	= 11.	NAHVE a safe place
REBUKE	= 12.	BEEUKR to criticize
PRUDENT	= 13.	PTUNDER sensible
PEERLESS	= 14.	LSRESEEP unmatched
MORTAL	= 15.	MLRATO a human
MODERATION	= 16.	TOMEDORNAI balance
LYRE	= 17.	RYLE a stringed instrument
INHOSPITABLE	= 18.	AOLIPNTHBISE unfriendly
IMPIOUS	= 19.	SIPIUMO lacking respect for religion
WIELD	= 20.	IDWEL to use

www.ingramcontent.com/pod-product-compliance
Lightning Source LLC
Chambersburg PA
CBHW051406070526
44584CB00023B/3317